Conversations
with Robert Frost

Conversations ᵂⁱᵗʰ Robert Frost

The Bread Loaf Period

Peter J. Stanlis

With a new introduction by the author

Transaction Publishers
New Brunswick (U.S.A.) and London (U.K.)

Library of Congress Catalog Number: 2009042753
ISBN: 978-1-4128-1071-5
Printed in the United States of America

Library of Congress Cataloging-in-Publication Data

Stanlis, Peter J. (Peter James), 1920-
    Conversations with Robert Frost : the Bread Loaf period / Peter J. Stanlis.
        p. cm.
    ISBN 978-1-4128-1071-5 (alk. paper)
        1. Frost, Robert, 1874-1963--Interviews. 2. Poets, American--20th century--Interviews. I. Frost, Robert, 1874-1963. II. Title.

PS3511.R94Z9253 2009
811'.52--dc22

                                                          2009042753

Yes, there you have it at the root of things.
We have to stay afraid deep in our souls
Our sacrifice—the best we have to offer,
And not our worst nor second best, our best,

* *

Our lives laid down in war and peace—may not
Be found acceptable in Heaven's sight.
And that they may be in the only prayer
Worth praying. May my sacrifice
Be found acceptable in Heaven's sight.

A Masque of Mercy by Robert Frost

Contents

Introduction to the Transaction Edition

Perhaps the best way to perceive the importance of these conversations with Robert Frost during 1939-1941 is within the much larger context of our twenty-three years of friendship up to Frost's death in January 1963. These and other conversations provided much important knowledge and understanding that led to my publication, *Robert Frost: The Poet as Philosopher* (2007).

My most illuminating experiences with Frost as a conversationalist occurred mainly in his cabin on the Homer Noble Farm near Bread Loaf, Vermont. They happened during six consecutive summers, 1939-1944, while I was a student at the Bread Loaf Graduate School of English. After I returned to Bread Loaf as a member of the faculty, in 1961-1962, we had some additional good talks. We also met in Boston, Ann Arbor, and Detroit besides my occasional visits to Bread Loaf.

Frost once stated that next to poetry he valued and enjoyed "good talk" with friends who shared his deep commitment to poetry, the liberal arts, and humanities. Unlike his role as a classroom teacher at Amherst College and the University of Michigan, Frost at Bread Loaf was never a classroom teacher, so I was not his student, but simply a friend.

Our most common bond was that we both had memorized thousands of verses of poetry and shared interests in philosophy, history, politics, and religion. Like others who knew Frost well, I valued his erudition, intellectual brilliance, wit, and humor: he was without peer as a raconteur.

I kept careful notes on each evening's talk because I believed that what Frost had said, and the way he had said it, would be of great value to me in becoming a better student of literature and eventually a better college teacher. Originally, I never intended to publish any of our talks, and almost four decades passed before the University Press

1

of Mississippi published the first three summers of conversations in *Frost Centennial Essays*, Vol. III (1978).

My first awareness that Frost was a philosophical dualist occurred during the summer of 1939 when he spoke of poetry as the attempt to say matter in terms of spirit, or spirit in terms of matter, in order to find a harmony or unity between the two elements that constituted reality. He noted that everything has its opposite to furnish it with meaning. Over the next five summers he provided many examples of "things in pairs ordained to everlasting opposition." He explicitly named among dualistic opposites God (good) and the Devil (evil), soul and body, heaven and hell, justice and mercy, fire and ice, male and female, love and thought, liberty and slavery, rights and duties, and nature and art. In his conversations Frost frequently alluded to "the two-endedness of things."

Frost also insisted that it was impossible to make a complete or final unity out of the conflicts between spirit and matter. Ordinary empirical experience and rational discursive reason and logic were not capable of harmonizing basic conflicts. He held that the best method to ameliorate apparent contradictions in dualistic conflicts was through the "play" of metaphorical thinking and feeling. Metaphors included parables, allegories, fables, images, symbols, irony, and the forms and techniques of poetry such as rhyme, rhythm, assonance, dissonance, personifications, and connotations.

These were the arsenal out of which poets draw their insightful metaphors, but all metaphors were also the common property of every normal person. Just as a poem is "a momentary stay against confusion," a form of revelation for "a clarification of life," but not a final, absolute answer to the mysteries and complexities in man's life on Earth, so too—at their best—science, religion, philosophy, education, politics, and scholarship can be the means of ameliorating human problems.

As a philosophical dualist, Frost rejected the two forms of monism that resulted when spirit and matter were split apart into two separate, self-contained, absolute, and contradictory systems of dogmatic ideology that cannot be reconciled. In his essay, "The Transcendentalist," Emerson had set forth his belief that monism dominated the ways that mankind thinks: "As thinkers, mankind has ever divided into two sects, Materialists and Idealists." In our conversations over a period of several decades, Frost made it clear that he rejected both materialist and idealist monisms.

Materialist monism dominated Marxist ideology in politics, but in the physical sciences, scientific positivists—who made matter all in all—abused science into scientism. Frost observed that moral idealists such as Emerson converted spirit into an absolute good that denied the existence of evil. He said of Emerson, "He could see the "good of evil born," but he couldn't bring himself to say the evil of good born."

Frost agreed with the aphorism that the road to hell is paved with good intentions. He objected to both forms of monism because each was "the attempt to say all in terms of only one element." Because each monism assumed only half of reality, its simplicity often led to "monomania," to a fanaticism that infected religion, science, art, politics, and education. Both monisms complicated man's "trial by existence" by creating ideological illusions that led mankind into major social disasters. Frost believed that during the twentieth century, the triumph of political totalitarianism in Russia and Germany was the result of a monistic view of reality.

These three summers of conversations with Frost at Bread Loaf, filled with his many original insights on important subjects, including dualism and monism, proved to be a prelude to my life-long interest in exploring the relationships between his poetry and his philosophical beliefs.

With the passing years, I became increasingly aware that most of Frost's literary critics were monists, quite unaware of his dualism, or that they treated it as of no importance. This fallacy was especially evident in Lawrance Thompson, Frost's chosen literary biographer.

In time Frost discovered that like Descartes, Thompson was a double monist. Despite many attempts to educate his biographer on the nature of his dualism, to no avail, the poet feared that his public reputation and beliefs would be severely damaged by Thompson. Yet Frost's philosophical dualism remains intact, and his metaphorical statements on how spirit and matter are related in man's view of reality still provide valuable insights to every person's "trial by existence."

Peter J. Stanlis

Robert Frost, on the porch of Little Theater, Bread Loaf, 1940

A Prelude to Bread Loaf: 1937-1939

"The strength of the hills is His also." On September 18, 1938, toward early sunset, I stood before the Middlebury College Mead Memorial Chapel and read this Biblical inscription (Psalms, 95:4) chiseled in marble across the facade of its portico. The chapel, a Greek classical structure with six marble columns across the portico, was topped by a white New England meeting house steeple reaching toward heaven. In its Biblical emblem, mixed architecture, and Vermont setting, the chapel embodied perfectly the Congregational Calvinist origins of Middlebury College in 1800, as evolved into a modern, rural, New England liberal arts college.

The chapel faced toward the east and was silhouetted on the rim of a long sloping hill overlooking the gray-granite, ivy-covered buildings of "Old Stone Row" on the lower campus. Beyond these buildings, farther downhill, lay the village of Middlebury, shire town of Addison County, largely hidden under green summer foliage, but flecked here and there by the first faint gold of approaching Indian summer. From the northeast the dark green shadow of Chipman Hill covered the village. Five miles or so farther east the low-lying Front range of the Green Mountains rose three to four thousand feet above Champlain Valley, running north and south to each horizon. At their rim against the sky the dark, unevenly shadowed ranges were touched here and there with a purple glow, a gold and maroon haze, from the sun fading below the Adirondack Mountains twelve miles to the west, beyond Lake Champlain. To the northeast, past the villages of Bristol and Lincoln, Mount Ellen rose 4,135 feet above the valley. Six miles to the southeast lay the tiny village of East Middlebury, nestled against the foot of Ripton Gorge, along which ran state highway 125, the road that wound its way four miles through the first range of the Green Mountains to the village of Ripton. Three miles or so beyond were the Bread Loaf Inn and the Middlebury College mountain campus of the Bread Loaf School of English. The cottages of the campus lay on both sides of the road, in an open clearing of a large plateau surrounded by evergreen forests and mountain ranges. Almost directly north was the most conspicuous landmark from the campus, Bread Loaf Mountain, rising 3,823 feet high.

Standing there before the chapel steps that September evening I was almost totally unfamiliar with the geography of Vermont and the history and character of Middlebury College. I had arrived only the day before, hitchhiking up from New Jersey, to enter Middlebury as a freshman in the class of 1942. I had come up two days early, to find work so I could earn my way through college. Since the events that had finally led me to Middlebury had great bearing upon my college life, and eventually determined my going to Bread Loaf for eight summers, it is necessary to review briefly my earlier schooling and my literary experience before I met Robert Frost.

In 1923, when I was three years old, my parents had moved out of the "Ironbound" slums of Newark, New Jersey, where I was born, to the beautiful rural suburb of Nutley. I grew up in ideal surroundings and graduated from Nutley High School in June 1937. But the United States was still in the Great Depression, and my family had a very hard struggle to survive. Between June 1937 and September 1938 I spent months in fruitless searching for work. After making the rounds of shops and factories each morning, I usually spent my afternoons and evenings in the Nutley Public Library. In fourteen months I read several hundreds of books—much history, politics, and science, some philosophy, but particularly the fine arts and literature.

I read voraciously yet selectively in the whole range of English and American fiction, drama, and poetry. Since childhood I had had an intense and natural affinity for poetry, graduating from *Mother Goose* and Robert Louis Stevenson's *A Child's Garden of Verses* to the poetry anthologies of Louis Untermeyer used as texts in high school. I had soon discovered that when I liked a poem, often a single reading enabled me to retain it in memory and to quote it in full, almost regardless of its length. Later, when I came to know Frost well, he said my acute memory for poetry was the result of "out-of-school" and "self-assigned" readings, rather than "in-school" and "laid-on" education. However it may be explained, I read poetry in the spirit of what Frost in "A Tuft of Flowers" called "sheer morning gladness at the brim." Undoubtedly, Frost was largely right. The poems lodged in my mind because I read them with all the intense and spontaneous enthusiasm of uncritical youth, with an intuitional love, or what Frost called "passionate preference," (*Interviews,* p. 208), and not as a body of academic knowledge to be learned. During the fourteen months prior to entering Middlebury I read and retained in memory thousands of lines of poetry, from Shakespeare's sonnets, lyrics, and plays; from the poems of Ben Jonson, Donne, Herrick, and the Cavalier poets; from Milton, Dryden, Pope, Thompson, Gray, Blair, Young, Samuel Johnson and Goldsmith; from all the major and some minor Romantic and Victorian poets; and from the modern British and American poets in the latest edition of Untermeyer's anthology, including Frost. Among American nineteenth-century poets I knew to memory many poems of Bryant, Poe, Emerson, Whitman, Crane, Dickinson, and others.

Although I did not realize it then, I was really preparing myself in the best possible manner for entering Middlebury, for my summers at Bread Loaf, and for my conversations with Frost. But because of the depressed economic condition of my family, and my inability to find work, until Christmas of 1937 I had not entertained any hope of going to college at all. Then by chance I met a history teacher I had known in Nutley High School. About the middle of December Miss Esther Byerley found me reading in the library, and with the help of one of my high school English teachers, Miss Ida Cone, who had sent several students to Middlebury College, encouraged me to apply for admission. In February 1938 I was admitted with a half tuition scholarship. Through odd jobs during the spring and summer I managed to save fifty dollars, my total financial resources when I journeyed to Middlebury on September 17 to look for work.

The next day I managed to find four meager jobs—as usher in a theater downtown; as a page in the college library; as attendance officer in daily and Sunday chapel; and as a campus mailman, delivering mail and notices from the administration offices in Old Chapel to the various faculty offices. All these jobs together were not enough to cover my room, board, and books, and beyond these expenses I still needed to raise half of my tuition. But that evening, in front of the chapel, entranced by the magnificence of the campus setting and distant mountains, I had pushed my economic problems completely out of my mind, so that for a moment I was hardly aware that a man had come out of the chapel and was standing next to me.

He was tall, white-haired, and somewhat frail; he was well-dressed and carried a black cane. He had the dignified, formal bearing of a Victorian gentleman, and looked like the very image of a picture I had seen of John Galsworthy. He smiled broadly, shook my hand, asked my name and home town, and whether I was to be a student at the College. Soon we were launched on an animated conversation about the College and various academic subjects, and particularly on the place of literature in a liberal education. Newman's *The Idea of a University,* which I had read with great satisfaction just before going to Middlebury, provided the basis for my convictions. As we talked we strolled slowly down the long walk from the chapel to the lower campus, where for about a half hour we talked within the shadow of Old Chapel as darkness descended. Then the white-haired gentleman suddenly said goodbye and walked away. I was mortified to discover that although he had probed my mind, I had neglected to ask anything about him. I hadn't even gotten his name. I was acutely embarrassed over my bad manners.

Early the next afternoon when I went to the college mail room in Old Chapel to pick up campus mail for distribution, to my surprise I found a note in my box asking me to go immediately to the office of Dr. Paul D. Moody, president of Middlebury College. I went upstairs and gave my name to his secretary. To my greater surprise she recognized my name. She ushered me into the president's office, and to my utter amazement there stood the white-haired gentleman I had met outside the chapel. He smiled indulgently at my obvious stupefaction. Dr. Moody quickly put me at ease by assuring me that our conversation of the previous evening had pleased him. He wished to continue it and discuss some matters relating to my coming year at Middlebury. In the next half hour I listened and learned a great deal about President Moody. He was the son of the famous evangelist Dwight L. Moody (1837-1899); he had been head Protestant chaplain in the American Expeditionary Forces in France during World War I; he had met such luminaries as Marshal Foch and Sergeant York; he had known intimately and was a close friend of Father Francis P. Duffy, the famous chaplain of the New York City regiments of the Forty-second Rainbow Division; he had been appointed president of Middlebury College in 1921; his daughter, Charlotte Moody, had literary talents of the kind I admired, and had published in the *Saturday Review of Literature, Harpers,* and various magazines of fiction. By an easy transition from things personal to him to things literary, President Moody steered his monologue to the main purpose of our meeting. From fragments in our recent conversation he had pieced together the facts about my economic plight. He told me that out of his "President's Purse," a fund provided by the College for use at his discretion, he would pay the balance of my tuition for my freshman year. Before I had recovered sufficiently to thank him for this startling generosity, President Moody told me he had also asked the registrar to schedule me in the freshman English class to be taught by Professor Harry G. Owen. With that, President Moody shook my hand warmly, wished me well, asked me to drop in occasionally for a chat during the coming months, and ushered me out.

On the same day that classes began at Middlebury, September 21, 1938, a devastating hurricane swept across the northeastern United States, killing nearly 700 people, and damaging property worth tens of millions of dollars. Near Middlebury the hurricane washed out highways and bridges, stranding some parents of students for days. Symbolically, this regional catastrophe, and the resulting physical damage and dislocation of human lives, was but a prelude to what the whole civilized world was soon to experience in World War II. On our first day of classes Czechoslovakia capitulated to Hitler's partition ultimatum. Four years later almost to the day, I was to be inducted into the United States Air Corps at Fort Dix. Meanwhile, against the background of the politics and violence of approaching war, I plunged into the calm but intellectually exhilarating academic world of Middlebury and the Bread Loaf School of English, a highly civilized, aesthetically oriented, and idealistic world, peopled with scores of outstanding teachers, scholars, poets, writers, fellow students, and a variety of remarkable characters.

Soon after classes began I discovered why President Moody had steered me into Professor Owen's English class. Owen was a brilliant and highly articulate teacher, thoroughly educated in the fine arts as well as in literature. He had a catholic literary taste that included an appreciation of the best in Ancient, Classical, Metaphysical, Romantic, and Modern literature. He was intensely devoted to music and was a very accomplished pianist. Freshman English at Middlebury consisted of a year-long survey course in English literature, with reading selections from *Beowulf* through Thomas Hardy, in two large volumes. But Owen demanded much more than the rest of his colleagues. He assigned supplementary readings: a Shakespearean tragedy, comedy, and history; an eighteenth- and nineteenth-century novel; Boswell's *Life of Samuel Johnson*; and selected essays in literary criticism. He also required two or three brief themes each week, written on the daily assigned readings. By June 1939 I had written over forty critical papers for Owen, thus deepening, extending, consolidating, and systematizing my knowledge and understanding of English literature. Owen was a strict disciplinarian, and held frequent conferences with his students to improve their writing. Although I had entered Middlebury as a physics major, I soon shifted to English because I was more interested in people than in atoms and molecules, and Owen became my academic advisor. Before going to Middlebury I had become interested in writing, both poetry and prose. I had composed about twenty lyric poems, mostly sonnets, and had written some reflective essays. Owen provided great critical perspective for my work.

Before Christmas recess, largely through Owen's teaching and conferences, but also through the example of two other faculty members at Middlebury, professors Vernon G. Harrington in philosophy and Reginald L. Cook in American Literature, I had decided that for my life's work I wanted to teach literature in a college and to write. But the whole course of my graduate studies in literature, and of my professional life, was to be determined by Robert Frost.

In addition to his teaching skill, Owen possessed great social charm and tact and was an outstanding administrator. In 1937, President Moody had appointed him dean of the Bread Loaf School of English. (Several years later, after Owen became academic dean at Rutgers University, I learned from Frost that President Moody had groomed Owen to succeed him as president of Middlebury College, but that the war had destroyed this plan.) In January 1939, Owen offered me a scholarship and all expenses to attend the Bread Loaf School for the coming summer, in exchange for waiting on table. He reminded me that to teach in a college I would need M.A. and Ph.D. degrees and that going to Bread Loaf was the first step toward these academic goals. Owen agreed with the philosophy of education then practiced under Robert M. Hutchins at the University of Chicago, that a student should be allowed to proceed according to his proven ability and attained knowledge and skill, rather than through a piecemeal system of fixed earned credits. If I could handle the graduate courses at Bread Loaf, Owen argued, I should be able to earn credits toward an M.A. even before getting the B.A. He also noted that at Bread Loaf I would have an opportunity to study with outstanding English teachers from all over the United States, under ideal conditions, and that this would make me a stronger undergraduate English student. His clinching point was that I would meet Robert Frost at Bread Loaf and that after the summer school session I could stay over for the last two weeks in August and attend the Bread Loaf Writers' Conference.

But the hard-pressing facts of economics stood in the way of accepting Owen's very tempting offer. I believed it was essential to earn money over the summer for my sophomore year and to secure the B.A. before being concerned about advanced degrees. I discussed my problem with "Gramps" Harrington. He had taught for thirteen summers at Bread Loaf, from 1920, the year the school was founded, through 1932. He knew Frost well and had a very high opinion of the poet. He advised me to take the long range view, to ignore economics, live on faith, and go to Bread Loaf. I then consulted "Doc" Cook, whom I had come to admire as a man and a teacher. Cook had taken his M.A. at Bread Loaf in 1926, and he too was a good friend of Frost. He urged me to go to Bread Loaf, saying that the opportunity to know Frost was the greatest education in the liberal arts I could possibly get anywhere. President Moody reinforced the advice of Harrington and Cook and assured me that my full tuition scholarship would be extended as long as my academic record was good. He suggested that I apply to the Middlebury Inn for a job during my sophomore year; I did and secured a job that gave me room and board starting in September. I then accepted Owen's offer.

Robert Frost at Bread Loaf: 1939

I

At the end of my freshman year in June I remained in Middlebury and worked in the college library, packing several thousands of books in large wooden crates, to ship by truck to the Bread Loaf library for the reserve shelves for the summer school courses. Four other Middlebury students were also going to Bread Loaf: Edward Hayward, a native Vermonter, who had graduated and now ran the bookstore at Bread Loaf; Norman Hatfield, a senior English major, editor of the Middlebury College literary magazine; and Charley Sanford and Bob Maxwell, my classmates. Hayward had attended Bread Loaf every summer since 1935, and Hatfield had spent several summers at Bread Loaf. On June 21, a week before classes began, we all went up the Mountain to prepare the campus for the summer session. Ed Hayward and I spent a day unpacking books and placing them on the library shelves. Then I joined the other scholarship students, including some from Vanderbilt, Virginia, and Harvard, as a ground crew working under the direction of E. H. "Al" Henry. We worked with several Riptonites, Harold Whittemore, Milton Kirby, and a crew of boys led by Bishop McGill, to whip the Bread Loaf campus into shape. We cut the lawns, planted more bright flowers in the formal eighteenth-century garden in front of the Inn, rolled the three clay tennis courts and stapled down the tapes, opened all the cottage dormitories, did minor carpentry repairs on the porches, repaired and painted lawn chairs and cottage porch railings, piled firewood at each fireplace or stove in each cottage, and did miscellaneous other tasks. Dean Harry Owen was a fanatic for neatness, and when the Bread Loaf School opened on June 28, with words of greeting from President Moody, the whole campus gleamed in the sunlight.

Shortly after classes began, Harold Whittemore, Mrs. Homer Noble's adopted son, told us that Robert Frost was staying in Rip-ton, having rented a small guest cottage across the road from Mrs. Noble and her sister, Miss Agnes Billings. Harold Whittemore had a small greenhouse nearby and provided fresh vegetables for the ladies and for Frost. The poet took his meals with Mrs. Noble and Miss Billings, and often had dinner with Theodore (Ted) and Kathleen (Kay) Morrison at the Homer Noble farm, about a mile west from the Bread Loaf campus, which they had rented for the summer. But Frost spent most of his day in Ripton and slept in his cottage there. Late one day after work, Ed Hayward and Norm Hatfield went to Ripton to visit Frost and arranged for a group of Bread Loaf students to return for a talk the next evening. Like everyone else who had spoken about Frost to me, they held him in high esteem and stressed his unusual brilliance as a conversationalist. Apart from such comments and slight reading about Frost's life and literary career, I knew very little about Frost's personal life and character. I had heard that his wife Elinor had died fifteen months before (March 20, 1938), that he had barely survived "a nervous breakdown," that he had behaved very badly during the previous summer, interrupting a poetry reading by Archibald MacLeish, but that with the help of his Harvard friends, and particularly the Morrisons, he was beginning to build a new life. During the summer of 1938 Kay Morrison had helped Frost restore good order in his life by becoming his secretary, answering his voluminous mail, scheduling his poetry readings around the nation, and supervising many practical details in his life. Kay had given permission for the visit by the students, with instructions not to stay past midnight.

The next evening toward sunset, loaded down with half a dozen bottles of ginger ale, a large bag of ice, and packages of ginger snaps, Norm Hatfield, Bob Maxwell, two other students, and I walked to Ripton to visit Robert Frost. The poet, aged sixty-five, greeted us warmly at his cottage door. In a quiet and gentle manner, as we filed into the cottage living room, he shook hands and asked each of us his name and where he was from. Frost settled down in an old rocking chair near the center of the room, with his back to a wall. He had just moved to Ripton for the summer from Shaftsbury, Vermont, and there were books, magazines, and unanswered letters or papers piled on a table, and additional books on the floor. We sat in a semi-circle around the poet.

In physical appearance Frost was a rugged man's man, with white unruly hair covering a large, well-shaped massive head set on broad shoulders. His thick shaggy eyebrows hid the frequent twinkle in his deep-set pale blue eyes. His eyes were his most expressive feature. They appeared intelligent, friendly, yet a bit quizzical, sensitive, and crinkled at the corners with crowsfeet. His face was tanned by the sun, and slightly mottled, with wrinkles running across his brow and around his mouth, deepening when he laughed or spoke with animation. His hands were large and sun-tanned, like a laborer's, and moved about slightly as he talked. His dress was very casual. He wore light tan trousers and a short-sleeved, open-collared shirt. His voice was deep and throaty, slightly gravelly and gruff, and inflected with a salt-tinged New England accent. His manner was most informal, relaxed, artless, sociable, warm-hearted, and touched by good humor.

Frost soon established a good rapport with each of us, and as a group, for a spirited conversation. The same effort to charm a large audience that I was to witness many times in public readings of his poetry was evident here for the first time in his appeal to his audience of five young students of literature. He first asked each of us in turn which teachers we were going to study with at Bread Loaf and what we thought we would get from our courses. I told him I was taking Donald Davidson's course in modern poetry and hoped for the opportunity to read and talk about modern poetry. I was also auditing Perry Miller's course in "Social and Intellectual Backgrounds of American Literature," to learn more about Puritanism; and Mrs. Andre Morize's course in Elizabethan music, because I liked madrigals. Frost praised Davidson as "a very good man" and an excellent teacher and writer.

He asked each of us to say which poem he first liked beyond nursery rhymes. He appeared pleased with my reply, Robert Herrick's "Corinna's Going A-Maying." He then asked each of us to say a poem he liked. Hatfield quoted parts of A. E. Housman's "Terence, This is Stupid Stuff," but shortly became annoyed with himself when he got bogged down in the middle of the poem. I quoted Coleridge's "Kubla Khan." Frost remarked that Kipling had especially praised the lines:

A savage place! as holy and enchanted
As e'er beneath a waning moon was haunted
By woman wailing for her demon lover!

These lines, said Frost, together with Keats's lines from "Ode to a Nightingale"

The same that ofttimes hath
Charmed magic casements, opening on the foam
Of perilous seas, in faery lands forlorn

were considered by Kipling to be the essence of Romanticism. Frost said the lines have a strange beautiful unearthiness about them.

Frost then remarked how lucky we were to be "Harry Owen's boys," going to Bread Loaf, where literature was treated as literature, and not as a handmaid to something else—to linguistics, or sociology, or as mere raw material to study for "busy work scholarship." He said too many schools, especially graduate schools, took all the fun out of reading literature, by insisting upon a scientific approach to it. Fie acknowledged that scholarship has its value, and he respected it as a way of establishing facts, but it wasn't everything or even the most important thing for literature. In its humane treatment of literature Bread Loaf provided a healthy alternative to much current scientific scholarship. The teachers at Bread Loaf, such as Perry Miller, whom he knew at Harvard, and Donald Davidson, whom he had met at Vanderbilt and come to know well at Bread Loaf, were excellent scholars and writers, but they wore their learning lightly at Bread Loaf. During only six weeks, and in the relaxed atmosphere of the Mountain, teachers at Bread Loaf had to concentrate on literature as literature; they did not have enough time to spoil literature by demanding "research" from their students. It was a case of virtue by default, although most of the faculty were sympathetic with the policy of Harry Owen to escape from conventional graduate studies back into the true spirit of poetry. Bread Loaf teachers, Frost remarked, were more creative than critical and more critical than scholarly. We would get a good education by their presence, as much by talks outside class as by class lectures. Frost said the word *creative* was often abused, by being applied to a mere dilettantish interest in reading or writing literature, but so were criticism and scholarship abused, and never more so than when taken most seriously by professional educators. In approaching poetry he preferred the word *amateur* in its literal meaning, a true lover of poetry. A student should never lose his "amateur standing" in literature. Frost also praised Bread Loaf for treating both American literature and creative writing with far more respect than other schools did.

The great evil was the necessity of giving grades, credits, and degrees. Young talents should be free to disport themselves without too close supervision, particularly if the supervision was only to correct errors. A teacher's chief value was as an example to a student. He could teach by his example the superiority of leisurely ease and fruitful idleness over mere "thoroughness" and conscientious "busy-work routines." He could teach by his original expression of ideas the value of ideas in fresh relationships, not only in literature but in life. In the classroom, poetry comes to be too separated from daily life.

Frost mentioned that he had recently quit Amherst College, after being on the faculty there for years, partly because its structure tended to make the machinery of the college into an end. There were good liberal arts men in all the schools where he had been, at Michigan, Amherst, and Harvard, but there was also too much pedantry. Frost showed something like contempt toward the air of intellectual superiority assumed by learned pedants in having acquired some specialized knowledge through scholarship. He contended that to make subjects departmental, or specialized through one major interest, was contrary to the true spirit of humane learning. The very word *professor* was a kind of built-in affectation. Compared with religious prophets and with explorers, Frost joked, many professors had "little to profess," often nothing original of their own. They merely dispensed knowledge at second hand, about the original work of other writers, as book reviewers did. Even in what they considered "original research," or scholarship, they were merely "the first to be second." They were like the country boy who went to the city and picked up the current jokes and returned home and was the first to tell the jokes to other country boys.

Someone mentioned that he had read an article on Frost in an academic journal, in which the poet was called an "anti-intellectual." Frost asked: "What does that mean?" He objected that abstract "labels," such as being called "pro" or "anti" anything, were meaningless categories, without any substance. He asked, did anyone ever go around calling himself "pro-intellectual"? What he objected to was better called "pedantry," which was the "pseudo-intellectual" learning of educated fools who pretended to more wisdom than their specialized academic knowledge could support to any practical end in life. At this point in the discussion, amidst much pouring out of ginger ale into glasses with ice, I remembered and quoted an appropriate couplet from Pope about learned dunces:

> The bookful blockhead, ignorantly read,
> With loads of learned lumber in his head.
>   ("An Essay on Criticism," III, 612-13)

Frost nodded in agreement and asked me to repeat the lines. Someone asked whether the couplet was from the *Dunciad*. I said I thought it was from "An Essay on Criticism." Frost remarked that the *Dunciad* was a good guess, that there were many such lines in Pope's satire. He added that Pope was exactly right, that he recognized it was foolish to read poetry merely to acquire knowledge—even knowledge of the poetry. It showed ignorance of poetry as literary art to treat it as a source of knowledge, even though, as art, poetry provided knowledge of life stripped to form. History and science could more properly be read for knowledge as information, but poetry should be read for pleasure and insight, for a sense of form, for understanding and wisdom. Poetry involved knowledge of our total nature as man, and not only of our intellect, and therefore it went beyond rational knowledge. Frost denied that he was "anti-intellectual," but admitted that he was an "anti-rationalist." He rejected the assumption that man's reason alone provided the final source, or test, or end of human knowledge. Furthermore, he asserted that reason could not legitimately claim to be the arbiter of what went beyond rational knowledge, such as religion, poetry, and the mysteries of life.

This was the first time I had encountered the distinction between an "intellectual" and a "rationalist," and I was fascinated by Frost's quick follow-up statement that there was no contradiction between being a profoundly intellectual skeptic about the claims of pure reason as the original or ultimate source of knowledge and truth, and having a deep respect for human reason as an instrument for truth. But reason was only one of many vehicles for finding truth. And it was as subject to error as any other instrument. Indeed, often people with very superficial intelligence had the most exalted faith in human reason. As "rationalists," with unbounded faith in their own reason, they were not intelligent enough, or skeptical enough, to understand the limitations of human reason, and condemned as "anti-intellectual" men of far greater intelligence whose skepticism about reason aided the understanding and acceptance of its limitations. Frost clearly favored the full use of the power of the human mind in probing any subject—science, history, politics, education, literature, and even religion—but with a full awareness of where reason was competent and where it was limited. I thought he had neatly turned the table on the critic who had called him "anti-intellectual."

Norm Hatfield asked if Frost agreed with Wordsworth, who thought too much learning out of books deadened creative sensibility. Frost thought learning from books was good, but felt it should always be combined in good proportion with learning from life, which should enforce and invigorate each other. But it wasn't a question of the quantity of book learning a writer absorbed; it was rather whether or not he could use it well in his work. Of course, no one could tell beforehand what might prove to be useful, and a poet should acquire much knowledge. Milton was a great poet with enormous learning, who didn't flaunt his erudition. Frost quoted some lines from *Comus* to show how casually Milton assumed his learning. Milton was a learned, well-disciplined, Christian, Puritan poet. I added—as contrasted with Robert Herrick, who was a well-disciplined, epicurean, Christian, pagan poet. That seemed to tickle Frost's fancy.

We drifted into a discussion of what is a Puritan. Frost defined a Puritan as one who was willing to put moral bounds on what he wanted, including not only pleasures of the senses, such as "wine, women, and song," but also such things as political power. To Frost a Puritan was essentially an ascetic regarding pleasure and power. Puritanism was as much a practice of restraint through temperament as a recognition of and abiding by right moral principles.

I asserted that I understood Puritanism in quite a different way, as essentially Calvinist in morality and religion, and therefore not so much ascetic as anti-aesthetic. Monks in monastaries or religious orders were ascetic, and took vows of chastity, poverty, and obedience, but they were not "Puritan" in religious worship, because the aesthetic element in their liturgy was paramount. The Mass was an attempt to teach the good through a dramatization of the true and beautiful in Christ's life, passion, and death. The Calvinist reformers in Scotland and England were called "Puritan" because they "purified" Christianity by eliminating the aesthetic from worship. Their object was to be totally good, and they assumed that the good and the beautiful were antithetical and could not be reconciled. They believed the aesthetic originated in sense appeals, which were evil because the senses gave sensual pleasure, which led to desire, which led to temptation, and on to sin and damnation. Unlike Roman Catholics and High Church Anglicans, the Puritans regarded art not as auxiliary to worship, not as a stepping stone to the contemplation of God, but as a stumbling block which came between men and God. Therefore, the Puritans sought to avoid damnation by destroying the beautiful; they had invoked Biblical passages against the worship of idols and graven images to justify their destruction of art objects in churches and cathedrals.

My remarks were a summary of what I had argued in my freshman English course with Harry Owen and with Norm Hatfield at a meeting of the English Club. On one occasion I had gone on to argue an aesthetic theory of "art for art's sake," and in favor of a theory of "pure poetry" through the perfection of form and technique, totally apart from considerations of particular content or themes. The themes of art did not have to be moral. Hatfield had interpreted my theory as denying a place for morality in literary art, which he claimed showed in the poetry I had written, and he had dubbed me "the immoral bard." He repeated his phrase, as we argued heatedly. Frost listened to our exchange with great interest.

There was much historical truth in what I said, Frost commented, for he had seen in St. Andrews, Scotland, the destruction wrought to the cathedral by the Calvinist reformers. But he objected that my understanding of Puritanism was too narrowly historical and sectarian. In his view there were "'puritans" in every age and in every religious sect. It was not something begun by Calvin or limited to Protestants. Jews and Catholics were more likely to be "puritans" than Protestants were. The opposite of Puritanism was self-indulgent epicureanism and undisciplined selfishness. That involved a moral difference, not just a difference in aesthetics. Calvinism had created a special kind

of Puritan, and Frost admitted that many modern people identified
the word with thin-lipped, glint-eyed "kill joys." He also objected that
the Calvinist Puritans were lacking in an aesthetic sense. There was
beauty in their world, but it was centered in nature and the Bible, or
in simple art, rather than in the complex and ornate art of Rome and
Canterbury. I referred to a comment by G. K. Chesterton on this
point, that the Puritans thought it was better to worship God in a
plain barn than in a magnificent Gothic cathedral. They preferred
direct sunlight to light filtered through stained glass windows. Frost
responded that the New England meeting house had an architectural
appeal of its own; it was more than a whitewashed barn topped with
a steeple. I recalled the appeal of the Middlebury College chapel
and agreed.

Prudence dictated that I should have deferred to Frost's greater
authority, but with the rash impetuosity of youth I plunged forward
with a new argument. I conceded that Frost was right about "puritan"
traits being found in all sects, but as the enemies of Calvinist Puritanism had noted, there was such a thing as selective self-denial of sin-
ful pleasures. I quoted Samuel Butler's couplet against the Calvinist
Puritans of his era, that they were inclined to

> Compound for sins they are inclined to
> By damning those they have no mind to. . . .
> *(Hudibras,* I, 213-14)

And on the matter of moral self-denial in seeking and using political
power, I asked was Milton's chief, Oliver Cromwell, a Puritan? He
was a usurper; he had no constitutional sanction for sovereignty; yet
he had assumed a more absolute power than any but the most absolute
of English kings.

Frost replied that Cromwell was one of the great bad men in English
history, who accomplished much good by original means that could
be criticized. He admitted that Cromwell had a lust for absolute power
and that in this he was much less a Puritan than Milton, whose humane
learning circumscribed his will within common morality. I questioned
whether by Frost's definition of Puritanism Cromwell was a Puritan
at all. I thought Cromwell's lust for absolute arbitrary power could
be explained better by my view of Puritanism as essentially Calvinist. As one of God's "elect" Cromwell believed he and the "saints"

had a moral right to have dominion over the godless nonelect. Frost countered that appeals to scripture and theology were common on all sides in the political disputes of that age, and although Cromwell could be explained in Calvinistic terms, his temperament and character probably had more to do with his life and rule than the theology of the Independents.

At this point, in the new context created by our discussion of Puritanism, Frost reintroduced his earlier criticism of "pseudo-intellectual" scholarship by noting that it was not limited to college professors, but that some poets and literary critics had fallen prey to the same weakness. He instanced Ezra Pound and T. S. Eliot among the poets, and their admirers among the critics, who revealed a simple faith in a highly specialized erudition in dead mythology and personal symbols. He observed that the need of being versed in country things was far greater, and often harder to achieve, than the need of being versed in pseudo-intellectual myths and symbols. These writers reduced poetry to an esoteric puzzle, an intellectual game of identifications like "button, button, who's got the button?" It was a game that critics who liked to be symbol hunters loved to play.

Someone suggested that in an age as complex as our era perhaps it was necessary to use mythology and symbolism the way Pound, Eliot, and Joyce used it in their work, even though the use of such methods resulted in obscurity in literary art. Furthermore, mythological symbolism in poetry was the best way to capture the essence of our age. Frost disagreed. He questioned whether the object of poetry was to capture the historical essence of any age. That assumed that poetry must serve a social function, and such an assumption would likely land a poet into sociology.

But even if that assumption were valid, how was the present age best captured by a heavy use of ancient mythologies? Nature and the country were common and necessary to all ages, including the twentieth century, and provided the images and metaphors by which the age could live. The twentieth century was out of harmony with itself, because it had digressed too far into the specializations of urban life and had become much too remote from nature and the country. Frost noted that the trouble with the literary art of Pound, Eliot, and Joyce was that it was fit only for a "private coterie" of specially initiated critics. This process of excluding much of the reading public had been carried to the point that now we have critics writing poems for other critics to criticize.

Viewed vulgarly, as mere communication to readers, poetry could run the whole gamut from "most public, public, less public, least public, private, and esoteric." At the "most public" end were newspaper versifiers, such as Eddy Guest, who had no skill in technique, no ability to create images and form, but only a Sunday school message or sentiment to convey. But over the centuries most good poets have been content to be more or less public. They have been able to combine meaningful content with perfection of form.

Frost was all for a poet's perfecting his technique; the more perfect the better. But craftsmanship was developed in order to be "original" in the traditional forms of verse.

He again expressed his unease about academic life, because of the ways teachers treated poetry, as something to be studied for the sake of criticism and scholarship. It was bad for students to have their intuitive, spontaneous, amateur love of poetry displaced by such rational scholarly self-consciousness. Writers such as Pound and Eliot, and their academic critics, contributed greatly to this displacement process in our colleges.

Frost dilated on the theme that poetry should be loved for itself, as metaphor and form, as a craft to be perfected by those who write it, for those who read it, and not as an instrument for changing or reforming society. Those who thought that literature should serve society undervalued art and suffered from that great modern vice —an excessive social consciousness. What such people valued was skillful propaganda, not literary art. The Marxists carried this line of thought further than anyone, with their own brand of consciousness of what society should be. But at Bread Loaf, the teachers at the School, and the staff at the Writers' Conference, were right in ignoring the popular theory that literature and writing, to be good, had to be concerned with solving social, economic, and political problems. Frost referred to such work as "mad, glad stuff." He told an anecdote about a man who had recently told him that literature was good in direct ratio to its ability to move readers to revolutionary action. To which, with mocking irony, he had replied: "How soon?" Such men valued content or theme above skill in technique. Frost believed that form and content were both important, and should always be united, but the final judgment of a poem was in its achieved form.

He added that discipline in writing does not come from technical mastery alone; the theme also provided a basis for discipline.

Before Frost could develop his statements on writing someone noted that it was midnight and that since we all had to be up early the next morning it was time for us to leave. The poet tried to wave us down, to stay longer, but we were already on our feet, gathering up the empty ginger ale bottles, and moving toward the door. I was reluctant to leave and lagged behind my friends. When they had all filed outdoors I found myself alone with Frost. As we said "good night," he urged me to be sure to come again soon for "a good talk." "Come alone," he said. I was delighted and said I would.

Walking back to Bread Loaf we were all a bit intoxicated on ginger ale and the stimulating talk. I sensed that Norm Hatfield had a full head of steam over how the evening had gone. His pent up frustration and suppressed anger exploded. He said that he was disappointed because he had already heard last summer much that Frost had said; but he was especially angry with me, accusing me of talking too much, hogging the limelight, trying to upstage everyone, including Frost, and in general showing my special brand of freshman arrogance. I remained silent. This seemed to intensify his feelings. I thought he was right on both counts: Frost was reputed to repeat himself, with variations, from year to year, and undoubtedly I had talked too much. Hatfield threatened to cut me off from any future talks with Frost. I did not tell him I was to return soon alone on Frost's invitation. After all, despite our differences over aesthetics, I liked Norm, and really there was no point in making him angry.

After we returned to Bread Loaf, I spent several hours writing out the highlights of all that I had remembered of our visit with Frost, the subjects discussed, the arguments advanced, Frost's manner of speaking and appearance, and his pithy phrases. I recalled Samuel Johnson's advice to Boswell, that the important thing to record in a journal, beyond empirical facts, was one's state of mind and feeling in an experience. The chief value of keeping such a record was to note whether we improved in our understanding of life, other people, and ourselves. I recorded the evening's talk because I believed that what Frost had said, and the way he had said it, would be of great value to me in becoming a better student of literature and eventually a better college teacher.

II

On Monday evening, July 3, Frost gave a poetry reading to the students and faculty of the Bread Loaf School in the Little Theatre. After Harry Owen introduced him, the poet put his audience at ease by talking casually about some items he had read recently in the newspapers. His manner of weaving around a subject, making whimsical, puckish, off-the-cuff comments, reminded me of Will Rogers. His subject was the relationship between the federal government, Franklin D. Roosevelt's "New Deal" administration, and the poor in America. He noted that Congress had recently voted down "the Townsend Plan," to give federal pensions to old people as a means of solving the economic depression.

Frost remarked: "The test is always how we treat the poor." Then addressing his audience he said: "For Christ's sake forget the poor some of the time!" This remark produced a mild shock wave in the audience. Then, in a softly modulated voice he asked members of his audience whether they recalled where the Bible said that. Of course, he added, it doesn't say it quite in those words, though it means just that. He paraphrased Christ as having said: "For my sake forget the poor. The poor you have with you always, but me you have not." Frost remarked that some people think Christ believed we shall always have poor people among us, but the poet disagreed.

Frost disliked judging people by their economic condition or their social status based on money. He asked the audience: "Don't you think the poor are disgusting, and the rich are disgusting—as such?" If we must judge people by their "class," why concede anything to the Marxists by using "class" only in its economic sense? Why not judge people by their emotional or psychological class? "To which class do you belong," he asked, "the neurotic class?"

Most of the rest of Frost's remarks during his poetry reading were satirical thrusts at the Marxian view of man in society, which in modified form he believed some New Deal politicians shared to some degree, in their criticism of the American free enterprise system. Frost attacked the Marxist view of labor: "What some people call 'exploitation' I call employment." When New Deal politicians condemned "rugged individualism" and politically unregulated freedom in the economic sector of American society as forms of selfishness and callous indifference to the welfare of the poor, Frost refined upon the phrase "rugged individualist" and called himself a "ragged individualist," thereby insisting that he valued his personal freedom even if it meant suffering poverty. He lamented the great stress laid upon "social security" at the expense of private freedom. To live life assertively, with audacity and courage, Frost said, man needed some "social insecurity." He was particularly critical of Mrs. Eleanor Roosevelt, whose humanitarian sympathies for the poor tended to undermine the strength of character needed by individuals to overcome their poverty and become self-reliant. Frost remarked that because of the psychology of the New Deal, which aimed at eliminating failure through competitive adversity and establishing an egalitarian mediocrity, about the only social activity in which the desire to excel still remained strong in America was competitive sports.

Frost remarked that socialism was based on the same theory as fire insurance. If everyone paid a small premium, the risk of a total loss through fire by any particular individual could be eliminated. The New Deal socialists applied the principle to the economic life of Americans, in order to take all the risk out of life.

He observed that there were advantages and disadvantages in every state or condition of life. The disadvantage in being poor was that it was damned inconvenient. The advantage was that the poor had to face the realities of life each day, to survive, and this made them realists. There were no illusions in the poor, except when they became revolutionary theorists and dreamed of the big rock candy mountain of a future Utopia. The advantage of being rich was in the power and convenience money provided. The disadvantage was that wealth often weakened character, by making what a person has more important than what a person is. Few things were worse than having too much money combined with too little character or wisdom. Today we have a unique development—the growth of millionaire socialite socialists. Some of these Utopian dreamers become socialists more out of a bad conscience because of their father's or grandfather's success than because they really like the poor.

Frost interspersed these remarks with readings of his poems, including "Birches," "Provide, Provide," "A Drumlin Woodchuck," "A Roadside Stand," "Mending Wall," and "Stopping by Woods on a Snowy Evening." When he came to the final stanza of "Provide, Provide," a truculent and almost defiant tone entered into his reading, so that the final two words, "Provide, provide!" were delivered in a snarl, drawing out the long "o" and "i" vowels. He also read "The Runaway" and commented that he hoped his audience caught the urgent tone of "moral indignation" in the last three lines:

> Whoever it is that leaves him out so late, When other
> creatures have gone to stall and bin,
> Ought to be told to come and take him in.

Hortense Moore and Robert Frost discussing the dramatization of Frost's "Snow," on the porch of Bread Loaf Inn, 1939

Frost never commented on his poems beyond a few words on the occasion of their composition, or on how some friend "got it" or failed to "get it." Clearly, he believed his poems should stand or fall as delivered, without any critical comments from him.

III

On Monday afternoon, July 10, Frost returned to the Bread Loaf campus to discuss with Professor Hortense Moore, director of drama in the Little Theatre, the staging of his poem "Snow," which she had adapted as a one-act play. Miss Moore was directing the play, assisted in the stage settings by Raymond Bosworth. Students at Bread Loaf were allowed to sit in on their preliminary discussions, and I took advantage of this privilege, even though I was not a drama student.

Leon Drury was selected to play Brother Meserve, a preacher of the fundamentalist Racker sect, who is caught in a blizzard while returning home after preaching, and is forced to stop over at the home of a farm couple, the Coles. His insistence on going back into the blizzard, in order to reach home that night, creates the central plot and character conflict in the play. Brother Meserve's wife, an off-stage character who is contacted by telephone, wants her husband to remain overnight with the Coles, until the storm subsides. The Coles, who consider themselves intellectually and morally superior to Meserve, would just as soon not be bothered by him as an overnight guest. Mr. Cole was to be played by "Al" Henry, and Priscilla March was chosen to play his wife, Helen Cole.

After the cast was chosen they spoke sections of the play, and there was a long discussion among Miss Moore, the cast, and Frost on whether the speeches of Meserve were too long, without sufficient interruption by the other characters, for stage drama. Frost thought not. He contended that Meserve, as a preacher, was supposed to be a rather talkative character and that if the actors spoke their blank verse lines with proper rhythm, tone, and emphasis, there would be no problem. Everything depended on the actor's skill in the timing in his dialogue. The voice tones and rhythm of the actors had to create the illusion of "natural" speech. Frost also objected to the use of a heavy New England dialect. Even though the setting was rural New England, "Snow" was not a "regional" play. Frost argued that too obvious use of an unauthentic dialect would distract attention from the characters and the dramatic situation, as had happened in an American presentation of Synge's *Riders to the Sea.* Miss Moore was clearly convinced by Frost's remarks. But when the poet left the Little Theatre, he was apparently unconvinced that the poem as play would be well acted.

As Frost walked away, I caught up to him and told him I would like to accept his invitation to visit him for an evening talk. We agreed on the next evening.

IV

Around 8:30 P.M., I walked to Ripton for my first meeting alone with Frost. I was filled with a strong sense of exhilaration and anticipation. Frost's previous talks had whetted my appetite, and I was eager to discuss poets and poetry and all sorts of subjects with him.

Still smarting from Hatfield's criticism, I began by apologizing for talking too much at our last meeting. Frost responded: "Never apologize. Never explain." He denied that I had violated "the golden mean of grace" and said that as Americans we are democrats, not courtiers. We had met to exchange ideas and to learn from each other. I admitted that I had learned to see Puritans in another light. Frost remarked that I had defended my view very well. It was a common mistake for students to hide their weaknesses and cover their ignorance from their teachers, instead of having their ideas challenged and tested. That was because they were too concerned about grades. He said that good talk, like poetry, is one of the great norms for civilization. In conflicts of ideas we should fight hard with courage and magnanimity, to win for the ideas we believed in. Intellectual virtues and social virtues can be combined. Our wit should be pleasant and disarming. Socratic irony is a form of polite dissimulation. Frost admitted that good talk lifted him out of himself. His remarks not only put me completely at ease, so that I felt I could always be candid with him, but they gave me an important insight into how he regarded conversation, and its significance in life and education.

After we were well settled in our chairs, Frost asked me for more details about my family background and upbringing in New Jersey. I sensed how genuinely interested he was in what I told him about myself, particularly in the events that had brought me to Middlebury. He became extraordinarily alert when I mentioned the great kindness

and personal interest of President Moody. I told him I owed my freshman year at Middlebury to Moody and that he had established a base
for my next three years in college. I mentioned Moody's high regard
for him. Frost said Moody had a high respect for writing and a deep
personal interest in good literature and that he had once been an excellent editor, preferring professional writers to academic scholars.

Frost remarked that his mother's family name was Moodie, spelled
with an "ie" rather than a "y," and that she had migrated to the United
States from Scotland after her father had drowned at sea. That gave
him something in common with recent American emigrants, one gen-
eration removed from Europe, to balance off with his father's family,
which had come to America early in the seventeenth century. Speaking of his mother, Frost asked whether I had ever noticed how fond
the Scots were of the diminutive? His mother had used it frequently.
Where the English said "lad" and "lass" the Scots said "laddie" and
"lassie." Bobby Burns often used the diminutive: "bonnie," "mousie."
The Scots, he said, were a remarkable people. Considering how small
their population was, their achievements in history were tremendous.
Their stark climate and Calvinist religion had disciplined them to
work hard just to survive.

When they left Scotland their characters were strong, and they were
like a spring that had been compressed by adversity but was suddenly
released by opportunity. The Irish were like that in politics, and the
Jews in business, but the Scots were like that in many things.

Frost advanced the theme that strongly-formed character can carry
through several generations. Paul Moody had told Frost how much he
owed to his father. Frost had a high respect for Moody's father as an
evangelist. He liked men who held strongly to their commitments. He
was not concerned much with the substance of their beliefs but with
the firmness with which they held them. Life would test their ideas.
He did not care for such "scoffers" as H. L. Mencken and Clarence
Darrow, who had nothing to offer in matters of faith except their acid
wit and private reason. He also disliked college professors who thought
it their right and duty to destroy the traditional religious beliefs of
their students and replace their beliefs with modern science. Paul
Moody was a thoroughly admirable man. Frost was glad to see that
my gratitude was not mixed with resentment. He said some people
resent help from others because it put them in debt to their benefac-

tors. I suggested that I could discharge my debt by helping others as I had been helped.

I said I was as grateful to Harry Owen for getting me to Bread Loaf. Frost expressed his very favorable opinion of Owen as a man and teacher and said he had been treated well by Owen at Bread Loaf. He approved of how Owen was running the School, and how Ted Morrison was running the Writers' Conference. Both were among the best institutions in America. They were like the state slogan: "Unspoiled Vermont." They were like a modern Brook Farm, but without the manure to shovel.

I mentioned Vernon Harrington, my teacher in philosophy at Middlebury, whom I had come to admire greatly and who wished to be remembered to him. Frost knew Harrington well, having seen him at Bread Loaf many times since the summer of 1920, when the poet gave his first poetry reading there. It was rare, Frost remarked, to find an academic philosopher who believed so much in the moral virtue derived from physical labor. This gave Harrington roots in the earth, which was lacking in his model, Plato. Harrington was also a truer humanist than Plato, Frost said, in his intense love of poetry. Frost had heard Harrington recite as a monologue the whole of Robert Browning's "Caponsacchi," a remarkable dramatic performance of almost two hours. Harrington as a Platonist who loved poetry was as good as or better in his way than Edwin Arlington Robinson, who was a poet aspiring to be a Platonic philosopher.

I also mentioned Reginald Cook as a teacher at Middlebury whom I admired. Again Frost responded enthusiastically. He said "Doc" Cook was also an old friend of his, since "Doc's" student days at Bread Loaf in 1925. Frost commented that Cook was a fine athlete as well as a superb teacher. I told him Cook still held some track records at Middlebury. Frost was pleased to hear that I was active in sports. I told him I had broken the freshman cross country course record at Middlebury by two seconds, but had still finished second to an Indian runner from McGill University, who had broken it by twenty seconds. Frost said that Cook by his enthusiasm created enthusiasm for literature in his students and that for those who already were enthusiastic he helped to create disciplined enthusiasm. This was the true function of a good teacher of literature. A better appreciation of better literature would follow in time. Frost also approved of Cook's policy at Middlebury of teaching American literature separately from English literature.

Frost said there were at least five things a good teacher could have students do with a poem in the classroom: read it out loud; reread it; memorize it; write it down in an anthology of poems; apply it to life in a story or analogy with something students already know. People underestimate the importance of simply reading a poem. A good reading is as much a performing art as playing music or acting on the stage. If we miss too much the first time, we should read a poem again. The one thing a teacher should never do is analyze a poem scientifically. Never "study" a poem. Never put it under a microscope or magnifying glass. That is horrendous. It is like explaining a joke. That kills the poem.

Frost observed that I had done very well in my friendships at Middlebury. Four such men as Moody, Owen, Harrington, and Cook were rare in any college, and I was lucky to have found such friends. He remarked that along with religion, love, and poetry, true friends were among the best things in life. Next to poetry he valued and enjoyed "good talk" with friends above almost anything. It had not always been so with him. Early in life he had been very shy and fearful of making friends.

For the next several hours Frost talked about his parents and his early life and literary career, from his birth on Nob Hill in San Francisco through his return to America from England early in 1915. All he said, and a good deal more, was to be described in far greater detailed thoroughness by Lawrance Thompson in *Robert Frost: The Early Years, 1814-1915* (1966); and other biographers, such as Elizabeth Sergeant, also were to write about many of the points he made. But in July 1939 everything about Frost the man was new to me, and I found his reminiscences of the highlights of his life completely fascinating. I let him talk and interrupted only occasionally to ask questions on points he made, or to probe something further.

He described his mother's Scottish background, and how she had migrated to Columbus, Ohio; how she met his father, William Prescott Frost, Jr., when she came to teach at Lewistown Academy in Pennsylvania; how after their marriage his father went to San Francisco, where she joined him; how after their troubled life in California, when his father died, she took him and his sister Jeannie across the continent to Lawrence, Massachusetts, on "the saddest and longest train ride I ever took;" how his grandparents treated his mother badly, and forced her to resume teaching school, until her health declined and she died of cancer in 1900. Frost particularly emphasized his mother's growth into religious mysticism, from her original Presbyterianism to the Swedenborgian faith she finally embraced. He learned to love poetry from her. He remembered with great sadness his mother's stoical courage in facing the great tragedies in her life. Frost clearly loved and admired his mother.

Frost described his father as "a rebel," at sharp odds with his Calvinist New England inheritance, and a religious skeptic. While a student at Harvard his father gambled and drank. Frost said: "He was a wild one." In politics his father was a Democrat and sympathized with the South in the Civil War, not because he accepted slavery, but because his theory of political sovereignty favored "states' rights." Later, he named his son Robert Lee Frost, in honor of the Confederate general.

One of his father's favorite themes about America was the westward movement of civilization since the time of Columbus. He was fond of quoting a line from George Berkeley's "Verses on the Prospect of Planting Arts and Learning in America": "Westward the course of empire takes its way." The settlement of the American continent by the pioneers was so rapid, the poet's father contended, that it was "like unrolling the map as they went West." Frost's father was convinced that the geographical extent of the United States was too vast for it to be one nation. He thought it would split up into six or seven regional independent nations. Frost recalled that when he was about nine years old his father once spread out a map of North America and drew out the approximate boundaries of his hypothetical future nations. Although his father's political vision of the future never materialized, the poet observed, his regional concept of sovereignty was sound and consistent with the maximum of freedom for individuals in a democracy. Frost still believed in 1939 that for democracy to be effective the political unit of society and the nation should not be too large. As a "states' rights, free-trade Democrat," Frost called himself a "sep-a-ra-tist." He accepted fully the federalism of the United States, but he interpreted federalism to include a strong emphasis upon territorial democracy, retained on the state and local levels.

During the first presidential election of Grover Cleveland, Frost's father ran for a city office, and the poet recalled that he often went campaigning with his father through the saloons of San Francisco. He would put a tack through his father's political cards, and use a silver dollar to impel the card upward to impale it on the ceiling for advertising. Frost remarked that there was much "old fashioned political corruption" in San Francisco, in which an office holder pilfered public money. It was different from "modern political corruption," in which office holders waste untold millions of dollars of tax money on wild schemes, which they justify by claims of social consciousness. Instead of being condemned, as were the old fashioned corrupt politicians, the modern politicians were praised and reelected. Frost said he preferred the old fashioned political corruption; it was "more honest."

Robert Frost's cabin, near Bread Loaf, 1941, the first summer of the chickens

Frost's father greatly admired athletic prowess, and on one occasion he accepted the challenge of a champion long distance walker and won a walking race that extended over six days. But he weakened his already ravaged body, and his "consumption" and heavy drinking soon brought on a serious illness. The poet recalled that because his father thought swimming would help him recover his health, he swam out into San Francisco Bay, until his head was barely visible among the waves, while the son stood "forlorn" on the beach, in dreadful fear, until his father reached shore and crawled exhausted into his tent. Frost also remembered how his father would go to a slaughterhouse and drink the warm blood of steers, believing it would help cure his tuberculosis. When his father came to die he discovered he really did not hate New England, that at heart he was still a Yankee, and he asked to have his body returned to Massachusetts for burial.

Frost also spoke about his grandfather, William Prescott Frost, toward whom he had ambivalent but mainly negative feelings. His grandfather was the living symbol of the popular image of a Yankee Calvinist, stern and unbending in character and temperament, without humor, penurious, sometimes downright mean, and with no appreciation of literature or the arts.

Even when his grandfather did a kindness, Frost remarked, he always attached conditions to it. The poet recalled two such events. Once his grandfather offered to support him for one year while he wrote poetry, provided that at the end of the year if he had not succeeded in poetry to the point that he could support his family, he would give up poetry for good and take a "practical" job. Frost responded by assuming the stance of an auctioneer selling an item and chanted over and over: "I have one! Give me twenty! Give me twenty!" And, he added, it was almost exactly twenty years later when he published his first book of poems. When his grandfather bought him and his wife the farm in Derry, New Hampshire, it was on condition that he would live on it and not sell it for at least ten years. To insure this his grandfather kept the title deed until his death.

The most remarkable thing about Frost's personal reminiscences was not what he said about his mother, father, and grandfather, but his almost total omission of anything about his wife and children. In July 1939 it was still too painful for him to speak about his immediate family.

After Frost had skimmed lightly over his schooling in Lawrence High School, and at Dartmouth College and Harvard, and his years on the farm in Derry, he described how he and his family had gone to Britain in 1912, in his great final effort to become recognized as a poet. I asked him whether he had met any poets during his stay in England. He began his story with an account of his visit early in January 1913 to Harold Monro's poetry bookshop in Kensington, London. Monro's bookshop was "a gathering place" for clannish Scotsmen living in London, and a magnet for young would-be poets. Monro edited and sold copies of a poetry review, as well as books of poetry and criticism. His shop was also a forum for poets to read their poetry in public. Frost first went there out of curiosity. He arrived late and barely found room to sit on the stairs. Sitting next to him was a pleasant young Englishman who identified Frost as an American. Frost asked him how he knew he was an American. The Englishman replied, by his square-toed shoes. The Englishman introduced himself as Frank Flint. He asked Frost whether he wrote poetry and was pleased to learn that *A Boy's Will* was about to appear. Flint asked Frost if he knew his fellow American poet, Ezra Pound. Frost confessed he had never even heard of Pound. Flint laughed heartily and cautioned Frost never to let Pound hear him say that. Flint had recently published a book of poems, and he knew Pound and his "imagiste" friends Hilda Doolittle, Richard Aldington, and others, yet he was quite independent of them. Frost took an immediate strong liking to Flint. He told his new English friend that in his poetry he put far more stress on "cadence and metaphor" than on images alone, and he admitted to a strong dislike of vers libre, preferring traditional stanza forms and rhyme. Flint told Frost he would tell Pound about him and would arrange for them to meet.

Very shortly Frost received through the mail a postcard with Pound's address printed on it and a scrawled phrase, "At home sometimes." He put the card in his wallet and deliberately forgot about it for almost a month. One day while walking through Kensington he noticed a street sign and remembered it was the street where Pound lived. He went to Pound's apartment and found him in. Frost said he had expected an old and patriarchical man, because Pound had already published four books of poetry; he was established as an important literary figure in London; and he was known to be the European editor of Harriet

Monroe's *Poetry: A Magazine of Verse,* established just three months earlier, in October 1912, in Chicago. Therefore, Frost was surprised that Pound proved to be his junior by eleven years. Pound was by nature and art a kind of wild, Goliardic, modern Bohemian poet; this was reflected in his reddish hair, blooming unkempt, circumscribing the fine frenzy of his luminous eyes and neat red beard. At his first meeting with Frost he wore an oriental kimona.

The two outstanding qualities of Pound, according to Frost, were his sharp mind and his great ego. Frost referred to Pound as "the great I am, the perpendicular pronoun." Yet he respected Pound's complete devotion to poetry. Pound was clearly miffed that Frost had taken his own sweet time to call. When he learned that *A Boy's Will* was being bound at David Nutt's, he insisted on going to the printer's office immediately. They returned to Pound's apartment with a copy of the page proofs of Frost's poems, the first the poet had ever seen. He was embarrassed by Pound's reading his poems in his presence. At one point, Frost recalled, Pound looked up and said with relish, "You don't mind if we like this?" He used the editorial "we." Pound then gave him copies of his two most recent books of poetry, dismissed him curtly, and told him he had to write a book review. The review turned out to be of *A Boy's Will,* and appeared in *Poetry* in May 1913. It was the first important review by a major American writer in the United States of a book of poems by Frost. On the strength of that review, Frost remarked, Pound always claimed afterwards that he had "discovered" Frost as a poet.

But then and thereafter Frost clearly took exception to Pound's claim. Despite Pound's generous interest and apparently good intentions, Frost was more appalled than pleased by portions of the review. It contained a gratuitous attack on the boorish stupidity of American editors of serious literary journals for their neglect of Frost. Since the poet was then taking pains to cultivate the good will of such editors, he did not relish Pound's comments. Also, apparently taking his cue from something Frost had said, Pound painted his grandfather and his uncle as misers who had neglected him for writing poetry. Finally, Pound had clearly misunderstood Frost's character and his work. He thought Frost was a simple American farmer with a motherwit knack for rhyming, a kind of artless and undesigning primitive poet.

Even before the review appeared, Frost said, he perceived that Pound wished to "expropriate" him for his own literary interests, by sponsoring him among literary people in London. Through Pound he met William Butler Yeats, whose poetry and plays Frost had long known, and whom he regarded as the greatest living poet in Britain. Pound and Flint told him that Yeats thought *A Boy's Will* was the best book of poetry to come out of America in many years. But Frost found Yeats was almost as vain and egocentric as Pound, and as "daft on spiritualism" as Pound was on wild experimentation in verse techniques. Frost saw Yeats several times, but always in the presence of a crowd of admirers of his poetry, or of other spiritualists, and they never became friendly. Years later, Frost remarked rather tartly, after the Irish Republic was established, Yeats became dissatisfied because he was made a mere senator, when he expected much more, and he spent his later years anxiously maintaining his various "masks" as a public man, rather than writing poetry. In describing Yeats's attempts to attract admirers late in life, Frost compared him to a piece of sticky candy left in the sun, drawing flies.

In several meetings with Pound, Frost recalled, they discussed the state of poetry in America. Pound considered the United States a cultural wasteland and was already a permanent expatriate. Since Frost was American to the marrow of his bones, even though his country was far from being aesthetically oriented as he wished, he differed strongly from Pound in his affection for America. Pound praised William Carlos Williams as the best poet in America and urged Frost to look him up when he returned. Frost also remembered how he and Pound chortled heartily over Robinson's lines in "Miniver Cheevy":

> Miniver thought, and thought, and thought,
>   And thought about it.

The fourth "thought," Frost said, was the marvelous excess that overflowed and made the lines leap beyond prose into poetry. Even in retrospect, while quoting the lines, Frost laughed with glee.

But Pound's character and erratic temperament were not congenial to Frost. He remarked that when Pound's son was born he named him Homer Shakespeare Pound, "for the crescendo effect." Once when the two poets had dinner together in a London restaurant, Pound quoted his poems so loudly, and used such vulgar language, that their waiter placed a tall screen around their table. Frost also repeated a story told him by some English literary friends—that after Pound published *Personae* his friends gave a party to celebrate the occasion, and as guest of honor Pound arrived very late, dressed in an old sloppy sweater, and insulted his hosts. Pound would do anything to be "the center of distraction." Pound thought of himself as not only the foremost poet of his age, but also as a sponsor of young writers, with wealthy people he knew as patrons to provide the money for publishing books and journals. But Pound's literary enthusiasms were like fads in fashions. When Frost knew him, he was about to chuck free verse and imagism for another experiment called vorticism. Frost recalled that when Pound once asked him what he thought about a poem in *Ripostes,* and he made some favorable remarks about it, Pound expressed haughty disdain toward his own poem, and claimed he had far outgrown it. By indulging in increasingly esoteric experimentation in techniques, Frost remarked, Pound eventually reduced his reading public to "a couple of fat English duchesses." Pound went into rages against the conventional sentimental and mellifluous lyric poetry of Swinburne and A. E. Housman. He was "full of Pound and fury" against them. To a large extent Frost agreed with Pound's strictures as they applied to meter and rhyme, but he defended the traditional forms of poetry against Pound's free verse.

But their differences were not literary; they were personal. Frost was not ungrateful for what Pound had tried to do in promoting him, but he was determined to remain true to himself and to his own conception of poetry. For this and other reasons there was soon a cooling off period between them. Shortly afterwards, when Frost came to know some of the "Georgian poets," such as W. W. Gibson, Lascelles Abercrombie, and Edward Thomas, he moved to "the west country," in Gloucestershire, and he and Pound drifted apart.

When Frost had completed describing his return with his family to America from England, I suddenly realized it was past midnight and I feared I had overstayed my welcome. Without apology or explanation I said I should go back to Bread Loaf. Frost waved me down. He asked if I wrote poetry. I told him I had written some lyrics but that my ambition was not to be a poet but to teach in a college and to write. I had submitted a dozen poems in a poetry contest last fall at

Middlebury and had won a prize of $25 for two sonnets. To celebrate I had spent $10 on a barrel of beer for the students in my dormitory. Frost smiled and asked me to say the poems. He remarked that my sonnets were smooth, too smoothly facile; the lines were too regularly iambic and run-on, without sufficient compression through rhythm breaking across the meter. He said that developing as a poet was like playing a game of "He can do little who can't do that." When he taught English at Pinkerton Academy he once asked his students to write on something they once believed but no longer believed. One student, who Frost thought was rather dull, without imagination, wrote that when he was around nine years old he used to think the trees along the shore of a nearby pond were palm trees along the shore of Florida. That was the most original thought this boy ever expressed in Frost's class. "He can do little who can't do that." Another boy once described a stoical schoolmate: "He's the kind of boy who wounds with his shield." Said Frost: "He can do little who can't do that." Thus it is with poetry. It begins with very simple analogies or metaphors, like those contained in Mother Goose, and it grows and becomes extended into more and more complex metaphors, until it includes the most profound philosophical thought that human nature is capable of reaching.

Frost went on. As metaphor, poetry consists of saying one thing in terms of another. The highest human thought among our greatest poets consists of saying spirit in terms of matter. That is the greatest attempt that ever failed. I asked, "Must it fail?" Frost replied that it must fail because men are imperfect, because the conditions of human life are too imperfect, and because language as a vehicle for saying spirit in terms of matter is inadequate. He said: "I'm always looking for a poem I didn't write." Frost added that his favorite figure of speech was synecdoche, because he most loved figures in which a part stood for the whole, or the whole suggested a specific part. As a poet he was "a synecdochist." New England was for him a synecdoche for the whole world. That was why critics who referred to him as "a regionalist" were talking nonsense. Wordsworth's poetry was not limited in its significance to the English Lake Country. Faulkner's fiction was not limited to the South. The concrete-particular suggests the general-universal. To illustrate this quality in the synecdoche as a figure of speech Frost quoted the first four lines of William Blake's "Auguries of Innocence":

> To see a world in a grain of sand
> And a Heaven in a wild flower,
> Hold Infinity in the palm of your hand
> And Eternity in an hour.

But a synecdoche doesn't merely compare two things, such as a part and the whole; it illuminates things, by saying the unknown in terms of the known. In saying spirit in terms of matter, the strange and mysterious are drawn within the orbit of the familiar and common, so that in writing and reading poetry we go "from sight to insight, from sense to essence, from the physical to the metaphysical." To illustrate this principle and power of poetry, Frost quoted the second quatrain of Shakespeare's sonnet cxvi:

> O, no! it is an ever-fixed mark
> That looks on tempests and is never shaken;
> It is the star to every wand'ring bark,
> Whose worth's unknown, although his heighth be taken.

The final line, said Frost, is one of the triumphs of English poetry. It describes the guiding star in its mystery as value, the star in heaven as seen by lovers and poets; and it qualifies this by seeing the star in the sky as precisely measured matter in space, as seen by physicists and astronomers. The line is one of Shakespeare's most profound insights, combining spirit and matter, and also separating spirit as value from matter as measurable quantity. Shakespeare understood the limits of science in penetrating matter. Poetry is more inclusive than science because it can deal with both spirit and matter.

Speaking of the human spirit, Frost quoted a line from Shakespeare's sonnet xxix, "With what I most enjoy contented least," as perhaps the harshest line of self-criticism of the spirit of man in all English poetry. He remarked that it has "all the animus of Housman" in it, but it is directed against the self rather than against the world, and is therefore on a much higher moral level than anything found in Housman's poems.

Frost concluded his examples of how the synecdoche works in poetry by quoting the speech of Jaques in act II, scene 7 (11. 139-66), in Shakespeare's *As You Like It,* beginning

> All the world's a stage,
> And all the men and women merely players.

It was a perfect example of saying a part for the whole, of saying the stages in the life of man in terms of the drama. Frost particularly relished the line describing the infant, as "Mewling and puking in the nurse's arms," saying that in one line Shakespeare had captured the first year of everyone's life.

We got into the subject of the creative process of the poet or artist, and I mentioned that Sheldon Cheney was speaking that night at Bread Loaf on "Expressionism in Modern Art." Frost objected to the popular idea that the artist is primarily concerned with "self-expression." That was a one-way street from the writer's ego, just as "communication" was a one-way street to the reader. I suggested that if writing is not centered in "self-expression," or in "communication," then it must be primarily concerned, as Aristotle had said, with "an imitation of life." Frost responded that the *product* of art might in some ways "imitate" or "reflect" life, though he doubted whether that was an adequate concept of its nature or function, but the *process* of creating poetry was better described as "a correspondence" between the poet and his reader. Creativity involved response in the writer and counterresponse in the reader, eye to eye and mind to mind. It was a two-way flow between poet and reader of sensations, impressions, images, associations, ideas.

Frost added that the writing process involved both the conscious mind and the unconscious mind. Poor writers are unconscious when they should be conscious, and conscious when they should be unconscious. Edgar Allen Poe had put forth a theory of creativity that was totally conscious. He reduced the creative process to a rational and scientific formula that applied to mathematics but not to poetry. Poe was dead wrong. In contrast the Freudians make the creative process wholly unconscious. They are wrong also, because to a certain extent, a writer should be aware of what he is doing; it is not just a matter of letting the unconscious mind take over, although in fact, when the going is good a poem should write itself. A good writer, while writing, should concentrate on his theme or content, on what he is saying. When he is finished writing, the only thing he has a right to boast about is his technique and form, how well he has said it.

We talked for another half hour or so, and when I suggested again that I should go home, so Frost could get a good night's sleep, he again waved me down. Shortly after two o'clock I felt I should leave for my own sake, since I had to get up at 6:30 to work and attend classes. Finally, after my third attempt to say good night, Frost said he would walk a way with me toward Bread Loaf. We crossed the bridge at the east end of Ripton and plunged into the dark, tree-shaded road leading back to the campus.

The night was pitch black, with dark clouds obscuring the stars. We could hear the flow of water of the branch of the Middlebury River rushing by over boulders to our right. We guided our steps by the sound of our feet on the road and the touch of the grass at the edge of the road. Frost's voice came out of the darkness like a disembodied spirit. He quoted what I recognized as a deliberately modified line from Milton's *Samson Agonistes:* "O dark, dark, dark, amid the blaze of stars," changing Milton's last word, *noon,* to *stars.* I was startled at the dark, ominous, brooding tone in his voice. I remarked that the philosophy implied in Milton's line reminded me of Thomas Hardy's in his poems and novels. But Frost objected to having the word *pessimist* applied to himself. He preferred *meliorist.* He even referred to himself as "a one percent optimist." He justified this positive term because, despite the sadness of the human condition, as a member of the human race he shared in the extension over the centuries of knowledge as revelation, and therefore in humanity's control over life and nature. As Tennyson had said, man moved from precedent to precedent into an open-ended future. Despite the cosmic darkness that surrounded him on the tiny planet earth, there was reason for man to hope. But Frost said the idea of progress as understood by some historians and sociologists, of mankind moving toward a Utopian state, was pure illusion.

On the walk back toward Bread Loaf Frost did most of the talking. He seemed intensely restless. I had not sensed this while we had talked in the circle of light within his cottage, but it was very evident in the dark out of doors. After we had gone about a mile, we stopped by an open area and Frost talked on the laws of compensation in nature and in human affairs. His theme was that many things which appeared as contradictions were really only contraries that needed to be balanced out. Contraries showed themselves in the contrasts of apparent opposites, such as good and evil in life, and of comedy and tragedy in drama. But the contraries were each real in themselves. They were not merely the absence of their opposites, as philosophical monists and Platonists thought.

We walked on, and less than a mile from the Bread Loaf campus we came to a country churchyard on the south side of the road. We talked about death as the contrary of life, whether it was "real" in itself, or only the absence of life. The great unresolved question was whether death applied to the spirit as well as to the body—the problem of immortality. Frost said it was normal to love life and fear death. To relieve the Gothic atmosphere of the dark night, and Frost's dark mood, I punned on the popularity of country churchyards, saying that people were just dying to get in. Rather grimly Frost joined in the punning, saying that death is a grave matter. We talked about the "Graveyard poets" of the eighteenth century, Blair and Young, and especially William Cullen Bryant's "Thanatopsis" and Gray's "Elegy in a Country Churchyard." We agreed that none of these poets, except Bryant in the final lines of his poem, took death with courage and stoical dignity. They all wallowed in their miseries and wept sentimentally because there was such a thing as death. I suggested that the Graveyard poets were rather too fond of crying in their bier. That did it. Frost roared with laughter. And almost as if to confirm the change back to a lighter mood, the clouds broke to the north over Bread Loaf Mountain and Burnt Hill and revealed patches of blue sky, and some faint stars became visible. As we stood there silently we could see each other's features in the eerie soft gray light encircling the road and the cemetery.

We walked on in silence the short distance to Billy Upson's place, where on our left, parallel to the road, was a long stone wall. Frost remarked that "the caterpillar tractor man" would not mind if we sat on his wall. We talked and quoted poetry until the first rays of dawn became visible to the east over Middlebury Gap. I offered to walk Frost back to Ripton, but he insisted that he preferred to return alone. We shook hands and said goodnight, and I hurried back to my room and spent the time until called to work writing down the highlights of our night's talk.

I felt more exhilarated than exhausted. I knew I had taken part in some of the best conversation I had ever heard. Because of Frost's associative method of moving from subject to subject it was easy to write out the matters discussed in the order of their occurrence and to note the themes he had expressed. I made an anthology of his most pithy phrases and noted especially his distinctions in diction in making points during an argument. Our talk had been both dialogue and monologue, but it was not Socratic dialectic talk. Frost was a naturally brilliant nonstop talker, a raconteur, with a deep love of words. He relished and savored well-turned phrases in the way a gourmand savors delicious morsels. He believed in words as deeds. He was highly sensitized to every nuance in the shades of tone in ordinary animated original talk, and in responding he took his cues with an intuitive grasp of both the immediate and the implied meaning in a statement. He was almost compulsive in his energetic need to grasp life through language. Neither in 1939 nor later did I ever believe that Frost's talk flowed because he wished artfully to impress people (though he did impress them), nor as some critics suggested because he was a compulsive neurotic who feared being alone at night. Far from being artful, his talk was naturally unaffected, though reflective, because his mind was full to overflowing with ideas and images. This made his character and temperament extremely attractive to me. Although I was only nineteen and Frost was sixty-five, because of his enormous zest for living I never thought of him as an old man.

V

On Friday, July 21, Frost's poem "Snow" was produced as a one-act play at the Bread Loaf Little Theatre. "Al" Henry, dressed in his working man's clothes, looked most authentic to both life and art. The play was quite somber, but the audience laughed at Mrs. Cole's description of Meserve, "With his ten children under ten years old." One of Frost's great themes in his poetry, that in a dark and cold universe humanity can create a microcosm of light and warmth by which men give some response to life, was captured by Meserve in these lines:

> You make a little foursquare block of air,
> Quiet and light and warm, in spite of all
> The illimitable dark and cold and storm....

I noted a similarity in these lines to the theme and dramatic situation in "An Old Man's Winter Night," which Frost had read several weeks earlier at his poetry reading.

After the play Professor Perry Miller congratulated Frost and remarked of the acting: "Wasn't it well done!" Frost agreed and expressed his warm approval to Hortense Moore of how skillfully the actors had delivered their lines.

VI

During the rest of the summer school session Frost seldom came to the Bread Loaf campus. He played tennis several times, once or twice with Kay Morrison, but generally doubles against friends, with Kay as his partner. He played badly, being slow in his reflexes and heavy of foot, but his opponents were as inept as he, and they generally divided the sets between them.

Late one afternoon when I was running cross country on the road between Bread Loaf and Ripton I saw Frost as he was going up the side road leading to the Homer Noble farm. We waved a friendly greeting to each other, but I did not stop to talk. Late in July I saw Frost outside the Ripton community house, when a group of students from Bread Loaf came down for a square dance, but again there was no occasion to talk, beyond social chit chat.

One afternoon early in August I walked past the Little Theatre and heard Frost's distinctive voice floating out to the West Lawn. He had been invited by Professor Lucia Mirrielees to talk to her class on methods of teaching English and poetry in high school. I sat in the back of the room and listened. Frost's theme was what poetry suffered in being taught badly in the classroom. He admitted that perhaps poetry could not be taught at all in school. He defined three kinds of "accountability" in classroom teaching. In their order of importance they were: The accountability of a teacher to himself. Every teacher should take great pains to enjoy literature and thus make himself as educated as possible in poetry. As with the Ten Commandments in religion, all other accountabilities in teaching depended upon fulfilling the first one. Unless a teacher was himself well educated in literature, he could not hope to teach poetry well to his students. The first requisite was mastery of the subject. The second accountability was to the literature itself, to treat it as important, with love and enthusiasm. Teachers should show by their example to students how much poetry means to them. Frost warned against treating poetry too rationally, by critical analysis, or as a subject for scientific research. High school was no place for scholarship. The final accountability was to the students. Frost remarked that he differed strongly from departments of education which taught that students were most important and that a teacher's first duty was to stimulate or motivate students to "express" themselves. Many students "have nothing to express," and those who do don't need a teacher to stimulate them.

VII

Summer School ended on August 13, and one day was allowed for the students to leave the campus and for the conferees to arrive for the second Bread Loaf session, the Writer's Conference, which ran from August 15 to the end of the month. Although Harry Owen administered Bread Loaf for the entire summer, the Writers' Conference was wholly under the direction of Ted Morrison. Owen's policy for scholarship students at the Bread Loaf School included an arrangement for those who wished to stay over and attend the Writers' Conference. In exchange for waiting table, students received room and board and were permitted to audit the various clinics in nonfiction prose, fiction, and poetry. For six summers, 1939 through 1944, I stayed over for the Writers' Conference, thus satisfying my dual interests in preparing myself academically to teach in college and to write.

The Bread Loaf Writers' Conference was born during the fall and winter following the Summer School session of 1925, and it was the joint creation of President Paul Moody, Professor Wilfred Davison, dean of the Bread Loaf School, and John Farrar, an editor and publisher. The first Writers' Conference was held during the final two weeks of August 1926, with John Farrar as director. Ted Morrison was director from 1932 to 1955. The Writers' Conference was a natural outgrowth of the great emphasis placed on both creative writing and American literature at the Bread Loaf School during President Moody's administration.

The Writers' Conference differed greatly from the School of English in its personnel, purpose, methods, and atmosphere. The academic faculty and high school English teacher graduate students of the School, filled with Victorian respectability, were replaced by nonacademic professional writers and editors and by amateur would-be writers, tinged with a cavalier Bohemian spirit. The pedagogic purpose of the School, with its structure of scheduled courses, lectures, assigned readings and papers, final exams, and credits leading to a degree, was totally absent from the Writers' Conference. Instead, there were informal talks on writing problems and techniques, tutorial conferences and clinics in which a short story, poem, essay, or play, submitted by a conferee, was discussed in open meeting. The academic, aesthetic, and literary atmosphere of the School was largely replaced by a concern with practical problems in writing. Many of the staff, such as Bernard DeVoto, Fletcher Pratt, Edith Mirrielees (sister of Lucia), Louis Untermeyer, and Frost, had been coming to the Writers' Conference for years, so that the last two weeks of August at Bread Loaf was like an annual reunion of friends in a mountain retreat.

Robert Frost was much more in evidence at Bread Loaf during the two weeks of the Writers' Conference than he was during the six weeks of the School of English. Clearly, the Writers' Conference appealed to him far more than the School of English. He played tennis quite often, singles with Louis Untermeyer or Kay Morrison, or doubles with Kay as his partner against Untermeyer and various other players, such as Lesley Frost, or in later summers with Richard Ellmann. Frost's tennis matches with Untermeyer were a popular comedy of errors. He played with quiet, stolid determination, remaining planted like a mountain and moving only when he had to go after a ball that was already over the net. By contrast Untermeyer played as in an hysterical frenzy. With his pince-nez perched precariously on the top of his classically Jewish hooked nose, his receding hairline arched broadly in a halo of thin frizzy hair floating over his head, his swarthy brown arms flailing like a windmill, he was in constant motion all over the court. He would stand flatfooted at the back of the court, his brown spindly legs protruding like broom handles under his baggy shorts. When the ball was served he would rise on his toes like a ballet dancer, and rush in short, quick, jerky, erratic leaps in the direction of the ball. This sports comedy was played with intense dead-pan seriousness, because of Frost's intense passion to win. The poet was so competitive that when he or his partner missed a shot he would become surly. On one occasion, in 1941, when I chided Dick Ellmann on playing poorly and losing, he winked and smiled, and confided to me that it was understood by him and Untermeyer that if they won the first set they were expected to lose the second. Otherwise, Frost was not fit company for a day.

Very early during the Writers' Conference Frost gave a poetry reading. President Paul Moody came up to hear him, and it gave me a peculiar pleasure to see them talking together as friends. That evening I learned that Frost's private talks with friends were a kind of dress rehearsal for his public readings: he repeated with slight variations in expression several of the themes we had discussed in Ripton. He called himself "a synecdochist" and said that all poetry, and even all thought, is essentially metaphorical, in which a part stands for the whole. He identified "synecdoche" as derived from the Greeks.

He remarked that poetry is at once "self-discovery and discovery of self." That is why it is simultaneously so private and so public. "Self-discovery" could come best by treating poetry as a craft, through mastery of technique and form, and not through inspiration and "self-expression." He thought the terms "creativity" and "self-expression" were being badly abused. They led young poets to "sunset raving." Young would-be poets would watch a sunset, and instead of describing it they would express how they felt about it. "It's all oh's and ah's with them and nothing more." After a while they wouldn't even look at the sunset, but would continue to express their feelings. This was "sunset raving." A good poet would so master his technique that he could describe the sunset in a way that made his readers see and feel it. He would never state his abstract emotions about his subject. "Sunset raving" was often found in modern novels, those huge, shapeless, sprawling expressions of raw creativity. Frost was very critical of modern literary critics who praised "the Russian novel" in order to justify condemning American fiction.

Frost read several of his poems, including "The Bearer of Evil Tidings," and remarked that it had been inspired by a friend of his, to whom he gave that title, because the friend often told Frost all the bad things others had said about him, in order to be able to tell him what he had said in his defense. (Later, in a private talk with Frost, I learned he was referring to Sidney Cox). Frost read "The Witch of Coos." He described the woman in the poem as "an old style witch," in contrast to "a young new style witch," such as he had met at a dinner party recently in Boston, wearing a low cut gown and sparkling earrings.

Frost made the cryptic remark: "You can't talk about the wisdom of having children until you have had them." He went on to say there are two kinds of children: those who receive every advantage from their parents and society, by having everything done for them, and end up hating their parents and their country; and, conversely, children who are neglected by their parents and society and are allowed to grow like Topsy, yet despite every bad treatment stick through thick and thin and remain loyal and loving to their parents and country. The first type of child is weak and unhealthy; the second is strong and normal. The theme seemed to be that the soft life destroys character and adversity builds character. He applied his theme to politics. The New Deal politicians in Washington did not understand that their humanitarian policies were undermining the character of the American people. Frost concluded his argument by saying that the great drift toward the common brotherhood of man does not take into account the individual differences in men and that he would hate to live in a wholly "homogenized society."

Except for a loose associative connection, there was almost never any logical relationship between Frost's preliminary rambling remarks and his reading among his poems. A poetry reading by Frost was not a lecture but a performance, in which a theme or two ran like a thread through his comments. He would weave around his subject, seem to digress from it, then return to his subject, carrying new materials to it from his digression, by which he enriched his theme. He often gave the impression that he was thinking out loud and improvising as he rambled on from point to point, even from phrase to phrase, with pauses between points and phrases, while he visibly probed his mind, fishing out from some dim recess an original idea, image, or analogy, which became reflected in his face and gestures, as the idea, image, or analogy welled up inside him and spurted out of his mouth in a voice that also seemed to be searching for exactly the right word and tone to convey it directly to each listener.

After Frost's poetry reading he and the Writers' Conference staff and a few guests went to Treman Cottage for refreshments and some social talk. The Treman Cottage continued to be the social center for the Writers' Conference until at least 1944, just as the large common room in the barn was the gathering place for the conferees.

During the day, between sessions of the writing clinics, there was often a good deal of light bantering about writing and politics between Frost and his friends. He enjoyed teasing them about their latest political enthusiasms. Bernard DeVoto came in for some good-natured ribbing, and on one occasion, when Archibald MacLeish visited the campus, "Archie" was criticized more seriously as "a true believer" in the New Deal. In all these exchanges Frost exemplified completely what he meant by "education by presence." He dominated everyone by his personality, including his critics and detractors. He was always treated with a special formal yet friendly deference, not only by conferees who talked with him, or asked him to autograph a book of his poetry, but even by his friends. While he referred to "Benny," or "Archie," or "Ted," or "Wally," or "Louie," they always called him "Robert." Frost was so obviously *the* literary presence on the Mountain that in response to someone's complaint that too much attention was being paid to him Untermeyer conceded that Bread Loaf was "the most Frost-bitten place in America."

Frost was a friend of most of the Writers' Conference staff, but he was particularly close to Ted Morrison and Louis Untermeyer. Morrison was a good poet, an excellent prose writer, editor, and teacher of writing, and an ideal director of the Conference. He was an affable, kindly, sensitive man, and knew well how to handle Frost's volatile and moody temperament. Since his wife Kay was Frost's secretary, scheduling the poet's lectures and even managing his domestic needs, Morrison and Frost were very close throughout the year at Harvard University, and not merely during their summers together at Bread Loaf.

Frost's unique friendship with Louis Untermeyer reached back to 1915. By 1939 they knew each other's character, beliefs, and idiosyncrasies so well that they could take each other for granted as friends who could be perfectly candid with each other. Despite their very serious political differences they clearly liked and respected each other. Frost chided Untermeyer about his Marxian economics and politics, and Untermeyer endured Frost's defense of individual freedom and American capitalism. During the Writers' Conferences of 1939 to 1944 they formed a team in running the poetry clinics. Untermeyer did all the legwork with the conferees, but Frost attended the poetry clinics four or five times each week. During the sessions of 1939 President Moody and Harry Owen also attended several clinics.

At the poetry clinics Untermeyer would read a poem submitted by a conferee. The author remained mercifully anonymous, and everyone was free to criticize the technique, form, and content of the poem, with no holds barred. While reading a poem Untermeyer's voice occasionally sputtered out, but his wit and humor generally managed to put everyone at ease for a good discussion. He referred to the conferees as "a nest of singing birds," although he and Frost were well aware that many of the birds sang badly, that some were sentimental or crabbed, and that even the old birds were sometimes more concerned with staying snugly in their nest than in singing or flying. Much of the poetry read at the clinics was wretchedly conventional.

On one occasion Untermeyer read a sonnet and everyone tore it to shreds. It was full of clichés, sententious sentiments, high-flown rhetoric and inflated diction, and was in every way a poor imitation of conventional love lyrics. This time, Untermeyer said, he would break the rule of anonymity. He was sure the author wouldn't mind. The poet was William Shakespeare. Untermeyer had read one of Shakespeare's lesser known sonnets. There was a stunned silence. Someone asked to have the poem read again. Then the conferees gradually retreated from their severe criticism. They found many little literary gems they had missed with the first reading. Afterwards Frost and Untermeyer chuckled over how easily people can be intimidated by established literary reputations.

On another occasion Untermeyer read a poem about nature which was so poor, so filled with "sunset raving," devoid of images, and with so much jerky meter and forced rhymes, that Frost could not contain himself, and growled out some very harsh remarks. In an attempt to soften the blow to the conferee's feelings, Untermeyer was kind and compassionate. Later, Untermeyer remarked to a group that lingered after the clinic adjourned that his and Frost's responses utterly demolished and reversed their stereotyped public images. Here was Untermeyer, the supposedly smart-alecky, hard-boiled, New York Jew, being nice as apple pie about the wretched poem, and here was Robert Frost, the epitome of old New England, the sweet old man and most loved and popular poet in America, being utterly nasty and hard as nails about it.

One other event occurred during the poetry clinics of 1939 which revealed one of Frost's most important convictions about poetry. A woman came up to him after a clinic in which "meaning in poetry" was much discussed, and said: "Mr. Frost, what do you mean by 'Fire and Ice?' " Frost looked her steadily in the eyes and recited his poem, then said: "It means that." The woman looked baffled. Frost responded in conclusion: "If I had wanted to say anything more I would have included it in the poem."

One of the social highlights during each Writers' Conference was the softball game played in an afternoon on the boulder-strewn meadow on the lower end of the Homer Noble farm. The staff, the conferees, famous visiting writers, and occasionally guests at the Inn, divided into two teams. Great care was taken that the best players should be on Frost's team, thus increasing the odds that his team would win. Frost disliked having women players, so they were not chosen for his team. Conferees with cameras recording the occasion called forth his silent ire and wrath. Fletcher Pratt, who was reputed to have been a prize fighter, was generally the plate umpire, and his gestures in calling strikes and balls, and in declaring base runners out or safe, were histrionic, and provided many hot arguments and witty comments.

Benny DeVoto and Frost were generally the two outstanding players. DeVoto's rambunctious character came out sharply during the softball games. He would lay down a bunt along the third base line. Then, after reaching first base ahead of the ball, counting successfully on the ineptitude of the fielders, he would keep running to second, then on to third, always a few strides ahead of the ball, then in a mad dash home, climaxed by a slide that began a good ten feet before he reached the plate, with the cheers of supporters and the jeers of opponents ringing him around the bases. Thus, on several occasions he turned a soft bunt into a home run. Once in his slide to the home plate he tore his trousers from ankle to knee and had to play the rest of the game with safety pins holding his pants together.

Frost was always in his pristine glory during the Writers' Conference softball games. He played with the same wild and reckless audacity as DeVoto, as though he were an enthusiastic rookie trying to make his favorite big league team, the Boston Red Sox. Softball was much more Frost's game than the genteel games of tennis at Bread Loaf. He would have preferred to play with a hard ball, so he could emulate his favorite ball player, the rookie Ted Williams, starring in his first year with Boston. But in the fiercely aggressive way Frost threw himself into hitting, running bases, and fielding, a dimension in his character became very clearly evident: the game was played to win, not just for fun.

One incident humiliating to Frost occurred, which illustrated why he did not like to play softball with women on the teams. Frost hit a liner into left field and tried to stretch it into a double. The outfielder threw the ball in a long arching fly back to the second baseman, Laura Brooks, a hefty, solid girl, who stood in the base path between second and first, blocking Frost's path to the bag. As he ran toward second base Frost saw her standing with her gloved hand outstretched waiting for the ball to descend. He stopped, perplexed by how to get around her to second base. She caught the ball with one hand, turned around, and casually tagged Frost. Fletcher Pratt had run out almost to the pitcher's mound, and with elaborate gestures he shouted Frost out, waving him to the sidelines. Sheepishly, Frost left the field. To be tagged out thus by a mere girl was almost too much for him. Had the second baseman been a man Frost would undoubtedly have knocked him over to reach the bag. It was very difficult to play to win when women players required chivalrous behavior by their male opponents.

The Writers' Conference of 1939 ended on a very ominous note. Despite the almost fairy land kind of isolation of Bread Loaf from the rest of the world, we were aware that all during August a war crisis had been brewing between Nazi Germany and her European neighbors. Like other scholarship students I stayed over after the Writers' Conference to help Harry Owen wind up the Bread Loaf campus for its three seasons of hibernation. On August 31 the Nazis invaded Poland, precipitating World War II. A group of us, including Frost and Untermeyer, gathered around a car radio and listened to an account of the invasion, described by the Nazis' propaganda as "a counter attack with pursuit." The ultimatums of Britain and France against Germany indicated a major war. Untermeyer was very disturbed. He appeared more concerned about the fate of Soviet Russia than the imminent destruction of Poland. He hoped that in the coming war the United States would not remain neutral. Frost remarked that regardless of its sympathies the United States would have to remain neutral until we had a serious grievance against Germany involving our self-interest. On that political difference between Untermeyer and Frost ended the summer of 1939 at Bread Loaf.

Robert Frost at Bread Loaf: 1940

After the death of Elinor Frost on March 20, 1938, a fellowship in her memory was established by Middlebury College for a young writer to attend the Bread Loaf Writers' Conference. In 1938 Frost awarded the Elinor Frost Fellowship to Charles Foster, a graduate student at the University of Iowa. In 1939, at the suggestion of Lesley Frost, the fellowship was given to Mrs. Lois Squire, to attend both the School of English and the Writers' Conference. Her inability to handle the academic work resulted in a revision of how the fellowship was to be awarded. During the fall of 1939 Harry Owen and Frost worked out a plan by which students at the Bread Loaf School and Middlebury College who wished to apply for the fellowship were invited to submit poems in competition. These were screened by Harry Owen and submitted to Frost, who made the decision. I submitted a batch of poems, and in April 1940 Harry Owen informed me orally that Frost had awarded the Elinor Frost Fellowship to me for 1940. Owen confirmed this by letter on May 14, in which he referred to the award as "the Robert Frost Fellowship."

Late in June I went up to Bread Loaf and settled in at Gilmore Cottage. Frost had bought the Homer Noble farm at the end of the summer in 1939, and came up the Mountain in May 1940 for the summer. One evening after work at Bread Loaf, before classes began, I went to Frost's farm to thank him for the fellowship. He invited me back for "a good talk" the next night. I arrived around sunset, just as Frost and the Morrisons were finishing their dinner, and they invited me to join them in dessert and coffee, after which the poet and I went to his log cabin, about a hundred yards up the trail beyond the farmhouse. Frost's new dog, a small black collie with a white muff around his collar and nose, ran ahead of us to the cabin. The poet said his name was Gillie, which was Scottish for the servant of a Highland chief.

Frost's rustic cabin, built of large, smooth, pine logs, had a cobblestone chimney and a screened-in porch facing west and south toward the farmhouse and meadow below. From the porch we entered a living room with a fireplace to the left in the center. The walls were of rough tan beaverboard. To the left of the fireplace a door led to the kitchen, bedroom, bathroom, and utility room at the back of the cabin. On the right wall of the living room was a bookcase half filled with books. Directly in front of the fireplace were two lounging chairs; on the seat of one was a copy of William Cowper's *Complete Poems,* turned face downward in the middle of "The Task." A half empty jar of strawberry jam lay within easy reach of a large Morris chair to the right of the fireplace. The floor by the chair was surrounded by cracker crumbs. The fireplace showed the charred ashes of previous fires.

I sat in one of the chairs and glanced at Cowper's poem. When I looked up Frost was gone, and a few moments later he returned with an armful of split logs which he set in place over the iron bars. He crumpled up a few newspapers and thrust them under the logs. As he put a match to the paper he looked up and said: "Out West they think a man's a tenderfoot sissy if he lights a fire from the bottom, and a dude if he uses paper." He saw me looking at Cowper's poem and said that Cowper lacked what we were about to have—"fire." Cowper was too thorough; a little sensationalism wouldn't have hurt him.

Frost settled down in the Morris chair with Gillie at one side. He asked me which courses and teachers I had elected at Bread Loaf. I was in Reuben Brower's "The Classical Tradition in English Poetry." Frost was delighted and said Brower had been the best student he had ever had at Amherst College, and was acquiring an excellent reputation as a classical scholar. Also, Brower had strong intuitive feeling for poetry as a living art. His course, said Frost, was mainly in the poetry of Dryden and Pope, our two best poets in English in the Horatian vein. I couldn't have chosen a better teacher or course.

I also had registered for two courses with John Crowe Ransom, one in "The Seventeenth-Century Lyric" and the other in "Analysis of Poetry." Ransom had rented the Schoolhouse Cottage along route 125, between Bread Loaf and Ripton, Frost informed me, and he was looking forward to a renewal of friendship with Ransom, whom he had known at Vanderbilt University. Frost expressed confidence that these two courses would provide me with good occasions to read and

Courtesy News Services, Middlebury College, Middlebury, Vermont, Max Peterson

Interior of Frost's cabin near Bread Loaf, 1974.

talk about much good poetry. But he expressed extreme skepticism about the analysis of poetry. We murder to dissect. Frost expressed the hope that Ransom would stick to writing poetry and forget criticism. As a poet, Frost said, Ransom had a fine ear for sounds. In the long run he would be remembered longer for the poems he had written than for any and all the criticism he had written or would write. His poetry had much dry wit, but was too "hard," that is, unemotional, for popular consumption.

I asked whether it was possible to be both a good poet and a good critic. Yes, Frost said, one could be both Dr. Jekyll and Mr. Hyde, at least for a while, but it was an unhealthy condition. The critical faculty is too rational and academic, and no scientific analysis can do justice to a poem. Criticism, as such, is largely a waste of time. If there is anything more to be said about a poem after it is written then it is a bad poem. If the poet had wanted to say anything more he would have said it himself in the poem. Ransom would make a serious mistake if he were to shift from writing poetry to criticism; he would be in danger of allowing himself to become dominated by modern science and the academic life. Frost thought writing criticism could drain Ransom's creative power and imagination and ruin him as a poet.

Frost asked me whether I knew Mark Twain's story, "The Celebrated Jumping Frog of Calaveras County." I confessed I had not read it. Fred Lewis Pattee, a faculty member at Bread Loaf for ten years, up to 1936, had sent Frost a copy of an anthology, *Mark Twain: Representative Selections* (New York: American Book Co., 1935), and Frost had reread Twain's story. As an editor, Frost said, Pattee was "a mouse in a waste basket." Frost remarked that Twain's jumping frog story was the most perfect short story of its kind in all American literature. It was a poem in fictional form. The voice tones and sense of sound in the style were lyrical: "The prose sings." The timing was perfect and there was "punch in the punch lines." Frost summarized Twain's plot, of how the jumping frog leaped free and far, like a true champion, until the city slicker filled him secretly with buckshot, after which he was heavy and ponderous, anchored to the earth, and incapable of leaping.

Frost did not analyze Twain's story, but treated it as a parable. Before the frog was filled with buckshot he was like a poet, light and imaginative and capable of great leaps by a command or the slightest stimulus. But after being filled with buckshot the frog was like a scientific critic or scholar, weighted down, stuffed with ponderous logic and knowledge, but useless in the art of jumping. No amount of prodding could get him to budge. The chief virtues of the poet—imagination, fancy, audacity, courage, wit and humor, which created his originality, were lost. "No performance, no form." The chief characteristics of the scholar are a love of facts for their own sake as knowledge, thoroughness, accuracy, and systematic scientific method. Most scholars lack imagination and spontaneity and are "humorless and witless." Scholars are "too thorough, too specialized, too fastidious, too proud." In summary, Frost said the scholar sticks to his subject until he is stuck to his subject. He exhausts everything about his subject until everything about it exhausts him and everyone else. His knowledge clings to him like burrs caught in crossing a field. But the poet allows his subject to stick to him as long as he wishes, and while it is attached to him he shoots out leads from it which he is free to follow. The poet keeps up a fast-moving interest in his subject while getting the maximum benefit of what his subject has to offer. This is the difference between the scientist and the artist. There were dangers in absorbing knowledge beyond one's capability to use it well. But Frost conceded that the scholar was decidedly superior to shallow readers who merely skim a work.

Frost compared a poet to a man standing at the edge of a Vermont boulder-strewn field, trying to reach the other side of the field by leaping from one boulder to another, without touching the ground. Since the boulders are scattered he cannot cross the field in a straight line, as a scientist or expository prose writer would, but must use metaphors, analogies and figures to zig-zag his way across. Through his imagination the poet must leap from one boulder to the next and the next; only with audacity, courage, and skill will he reach the other side without falling to the ground or finding himself stalled with no boulder to leap to, never to arrive at his destination. And, Frost emphasized, there is no way to retrace his way once he has made his first leap or two. He will either cross the field or not. The poet is like God, who writes straight with crooked lines. He follows Shakespeare's advice that "by indirections we find directions out."

Frost insisted that poetry is a series of intuitional leaps, and is never a planned rational process. Writing a poem is like falling in love, a form of lunacy deeply imbedded in our emotional nature, which creates through the special character of language an intimate correspondence between the lover and the object of his love. The Italian words *amante* (lover) and *amente* (lunatic) apply well to the poet. To reinforce his argument Frost quoted a passage from Shakespeare's *A Midsummer Night's Dream:*

> Lovers and madmen have such seething brains,
> Such shaping fantasies, that apprehend
> More than cool reason ever comprehends.
> The lunatic, the lover, and the poet
> are of imagination all compact.
> One sees more devils than vast hell can hold:
> That is the madman. The lover, all as frantic,
> Sees Helen's beauty in a brow of Egypt.
> The poet's eye, in a fine frenzy rolling,
> Doth glance from heaven to earth, from earth to heaven;

And as imagination bodies forth
The forms of things unknown, the poet's pen
Turns them to shapes, and gives to airy nothing
A local habitation and a name.

(act V, scene 1,11.4-17)

Frost remarked that he agreed with the ancient Greeks, who explained poetry as a divine madness, a gift of the gods to men, through which poets created order in a chaotic universe. Homer and other epic poets invoked the muses for inspiration and guidance, but they never explained their poetry.

If we are to be poets, Frost remarked, there are two qualities we must develop: one is sight, the other is insight. The first pertains to the physical plane; the second to the metaphysical. The first is more important. We always begin with the senses and feelings.

In writing, Frost said, we should have something to say, and we should say it. A finished poem should be at once "sensational and valid." The sensational has a broad scope beyond our senses in our emotions: "It runs the whole gamut from tenderness to blitzkrieg." Frost suddenly shot a question to me: "What is the opposite of valid?" I replied: "Invalid?" Frost shot back, "No! It's wrong as false." I asked: "What do you mean?" Frost replied: "You placed the emphasis on the wrong syllable. It's not *in*valid, but in*valid*." He explained that in poor poetry most metaphors are not false but sick. They are "weak, flabby, out-of-focus." In using language metaphorically poets seldom hit the bullseye absolutely. Frost then said: "You can tell where the center of the target is by the number of near misses around the bullseye." Good metaphors have two kinds of appeal: they should be persuasive and appeal to our reason and sense of truth; and they should be charming and appeal to our feelings. "Charming and persuasive," Frost said. That is what is involved in being "sensational and valid." In writing a poem, he added, there is no such thing as a selection or choice of words. There is only one word—the right word. Every word in a poem must be the right word. Each word or phrase in a poem creates an emergency which the next word or phrase solves. I remarked that I agreed with what he had said and that I thought his way of saying it was far better than Ezra Pound's formula: "Make it new but make it true." Frost looked a little startled at my mention of Pound, but said nothing in response.

After we paused to have some ginger ale (I had brought two bottles) Frost remarked by way of reference to a newspaper lying on a table that there had been much criticism of Marshal Henri Pétain for collaborating with the Nazis after the recent fall of France. Pétain had been denounced as a traitor to France and was even charged with being sympathetic with the Nazis. Frost took exception to such criticism. He said Pétain had proven his patriotism and love of France in World War I. At his advanced age Pétain had no personal ambition; he was merely attempting to be a shield between the victorious Germans and the defeated French. It was a sorrowful task; Frost sympathized with Pétain and discounted the criticism against him.

Frost expressed wonder at the swiftness with which the German Blitzkrieg had smashed the British and French armies in northern France. But there had been much heroism on the Allied side, especially in the retreat to Dunkirk and in the evacuation. Frost said: "I can't think of anything more terrible than having to cover the retreat of a beaten army." I asked whether he thought the German victory over the Allies meant the decline and fall of France and Britain. Frost replied that we know about how long a man will live, but we don't know how long a nation or empire will live. He doubted that the war meant the end of Britain. They would fight on. The Germans were now riding high on their victory, but they had many strong enemies. Frost said he didn't know whether to admire the Germans as courageous or to condemn them as foolhardy, for taking on the whole world again. Germany would receive no help from Japan unless she went to war with Russia, which he thought unlikely. Italy was too refined by civilization to fight effectively for the Germans. He remarked that before the United States went to war, or even thought of going to war, we must have a clear-cut issue against Germany. He did not think we yet had such an issue.

I was most eager to hear Frost comment on other poets he had known and steered our talk back to that subject by asking him which American poet looked to him most like a genuine poet. He picked up my word *looked* and treated it literally. He said that "old Edwin Markham," with his long white hair and beard, his self-dramatic, oratorical stance on the stage, and his tremulous elocutionary voice, looked most the way the American public thought a poet should look. "Old Markham" was a funny little man. He wrote poems of social protest that he called "bugle cries" to the world's poor, to rise and revolt. Frost described him as "little boy blue blowing his horn for the proletariat." Frost doubted "Old Markham" had ever read Marx; he was only a muckraking newspaperman and sentimentalist. After he published "The Man With the Hoe," he made a fortune going around the country reciting it and his Lincoln poems. Frost said there were some good blank verses in "The Man With the Hoe," particularly the opening and closing lines. It was a much better poem than most social consciousness verse, which lacked variety and wit. There should be wit in every poem, and variety in the way the sentences are laid down in a stanza. Poems about the virtuous laboring man are labored. The proletarian poets were witless bores.

Frost remarked that "Old Markham" once began a lecture and poetry reading at Bread Loaf, in the late 1920s by saying: "Up to 1900 the world's greatest quatrain was Walter Savage Landor's 'On His Seventy-Fifth Birthday.' But in 1900 I wrote my quatrain 'Outwitted.'" He was convinced that his epigrammatic quatrain had eclipsed Landor's. Frost recited Landor's poem:

> I strove with none, for none was worth my strife.
> Nature I loved, and, next to Nature, Art;
> I warmed both hands before the fire of life;
> It sinks, and I am ready to depart.

Chuckling as he spoke, Frost remarked that Landor's quatrain was marvelous as poetry, but the first line was very humorous as fact, because Landor was so short-tempered with everyone that once in a fit of anger he threw his servant out the window and then ran outside to see whether he had ruined his flower bed. Landor loved "Nature," his flowers, and "Art" more than he cared to fight with people. He anticipated our modern pacifists by a century. "Old Markham" thought his poem "Outwitted" beat Landor's quatrain. Frost quoted it:

> He drew a circle that shut me out—
>   Heretic, rebel, a thing to flout.
> But Love and I had the wit to win:
>   We drew a circle that took him in!

As poetry this quatrain couldn't begin to compare with Landor's poem. Frost argued that any sensitive reader could always tell whether a poem was struck off in a genuine intuition, or whether it was contrived, as "Old Markham's" quatrain was. The first line was genuine enough, Frost said, but the last phrase in the second line, "a thing to flout," was false and labored for the rhyme with "out." The third line too was genuine poetry, but the last part of the final line, "that took him in," had the unfortunate connotation that love deceives.

Frost remarked that a much finer poet than "Old Markham" was Vachel Lindsay. I told him that Lindsay's sister, a Mrs. Wakefield, had come to Middlebury College last spring to read her brother's poems. Frost said Lindsay used to read his poems before large enthusiastic audiences, leading them like a football cheerleader by chanting all the passages up to the refrain lines, then signaling his listeners to join him en masse in a ritual response. This was Lindsay's idea of how a poet should reach his readers in a democracy. It worked pretty well for him. He was an evangelist peddler of poetry. I mentioned that Mrs. Wakefield had tried the same method at Middlebury, but there were too few students in her audience, and they were too self-conscious about shouting the refrain lines in the college chapel. It didn't work for her. Frost said Lindsay had a genuine ear for the tunes of poetry. He remarked that Lindsay had been gulled out of keeping the copyright for his poetry by his publisher, and instead of becoming wealthy he ended up in deep debt, and committed suicide by drinking a can of lye.

Frost had a much harsher opinion of two other Midwestern poets, Edgar Lee Masters and Carl Sandburg. Both poets were committed to writing free verse, which Frost deplored. He dismissed Masters as "filled with animus against his fellow American poets." This was evidenced in his refusal to be part of a group of poets invited by Theodore Roosevelt to visit him in his home at Oyster Bay, Long Island. Masters accepted Roosevelt's invitation on condition that he could come alone. Frost predicted that Masters' poems in *Spoon River Anthology* would not endure.

Frost remarked that Sandburg, like William Butler Yeats, lived a life of affectation. But while Yeats's poses and masks had become a second nature to him and were an unconscious "sincere kind of affectation," Sandburg was artfully and self-consciously folksy. The differences between Yeats and Sandburg could be seen in their poetry. He admired Yeats's poetry very much, but the man was really too much the natural aristocrat to believe the common people were admirable. Yeats thought folk literature was what the courts lost, the kind of overflow or scum inherited by way of the drippings from the king's kitchen. Yeats's appeals to the ordinary people of Ireland were those of a man who knew he was superior to them in most ways, and certainly as a poet. But Sandburg worked hard at creating the appearance of being a common man, and pretended that all common men were really talented, like Lincoln and Walt Whitman. He was more an entertainer than a poet. In his stage appearances he wore a blue working man's shirt, and he would deliberately rumple his white hair and strum his "geetar" while talking sentimental, infantile politics. Frost said his response to Sandburg's "New Deal-Fair Deal propaganda poem," *The People, Yes,* would be "The People, Yes, and the People, No." Frost said he would double the thought and halve the sentiment of Sandburg, whose brand of populist democracy was really popular demagoguery. Frost wanted to see individual freedom under the Constitution, but Sandburg wanted equality of condition under popular will. He attacked Sandburg's free verse, saying, "It's like playing tennis cross-country, without boundary lines or a net." Frost concluded by predicting that Sandburg would be better remembered for his four-volume biography of Lincoln, published the year before, than for his poetry.

I asked Frost what he thought of Archibald MacLeish. He clearly disliked MacLeish's New Deal politics and called him "a true believer." Frost said of New Deal politicians that they think all Americans can be adjusted and readjusted to all their innovations, and they're dead wrong. He would like to see the New Deal replaced with "a new deck." Frost expressed dislike of Roosevelt's "Brain Trust," particularly Harry Hopkins and Guy Tugwell, and said the whole fallacy of a brain trust was that it assumed that politics was primarily a matter of intelligence rather than of moral decency in the use of power. "Archie" MacLeish thought of himself as the cultural leader of Roosevelt's brain trust. But "Archie" strained too hard to play the public role of the intellectual liberal in politics and culture. You could feel the strain clearly in his prose style, filled with repetition and variations of phrases, and self-conscious pauses suggesting he was still searching for the right word or phrase even after he had gone to print. "Archie's" prose style was a pale imitation of Matthew Arnold's essays. The thing that kept him a New Dealer was his belief that love would solve all the world's problems. But misplaced love creates more problems than love or hate can solve. On MacLeish as a poet, Frost remarked that "Archie is too derivative," particularly of Pound and Eliot. He followed the latest literary fashions. The trouble with MacLeish's "America was Promises" was that he made it appear as though America was *only* promises, and nothing more.

Frost expressed great admiration for Edwin Arlington Robinson. He was "the melancholy Jaques of modern poetry," full of tragic grief. He was a patient Platonist. But his good taste and wit saved him from singing the blues like our impatient young reformers. Robinson had the sense of play even about human tragedy and unhappiness. His originality consisted of saying new things in old forms of poetry. This is much harder than trying to say new things by destroying old forms. Poets could no longer express forlorn, aching sadness by saying "She stood in tears amid the alien corn," because Keats had already said it. The poet must find new ways to say this eternal emotion. Robinson found many new ways, and he lodged some good poems where they would endure.

Frost quoted several poems by Robinson, including "The Mill," and "Mr. Flood's Party." I remembered several of his sonnets and "The Dark Hills," and quoted them. During a pause in our quoting I realized it was past midnight, and asked Frost whether he minded if I returned to Bread Loaf since I had early morning chores, and I suggested that I might return for more talk the next night. To my surprise Frost responded favorably. He took his lantern, and we walked together down his side road to route 125, the road to Bread Loaf. He remarked that he liked to make new friends, because he sometimes found it hard to bear the love of old friends whom he had neglected. After we had said good night, as I walked back to campus I reflected that one of the most remarkable things about Frost as a talker was that when we met again after an interval of ten months he had picked up the threads of our earlier talk as though it had been interrupted only the night before. Also, something appeared to have occurred to Frost between the summer of 1939 and the summer of 1940 to make him much less emotionally high strung and tense. He seemed to be far more calm and rationally cool than he had been a year ago.

II

At sunset the next evening I met Frost in front of his barn, and together with Gillie we went to his cabin. I mentioned that I had just bought a copy of "Doc" Cook's *The Concord Saunterer* (1940), an excellent little book, and we drifted into a conversation on Thoreau's *Walden*. Frost had a high opinion of the literary qualities of *Walden* and said that parts of it were like poetry in prose. Thoreau was a very keen observer of nature. Like James Thomson in *The Seasons* he wrote with his senses concentrated upon his subject, not like some writers about "Nature," who seemed to have consulted the *Encyclopedia Britannica*. Thoreau proved to himself and to the world how much of civilization he could live without, while living in it; Robinson Crusoe proved how self-sufficient and independent a man could be apart from civilization. Darwin's *The Voyage of the Beagle, Walden,* and *Robinson Crusoe* were, Frost said, among the books he most cherished. *Walden* was more than a declaration of independence: it was a story of high adventure and contained much moral wisdom about life.

"Doc" Cook, said Frost, was a truer disciple of Thoreau than he. I asked where he and Cook differed about Thoreau. Frost said he agreed with Aristotle that man is by nature a social animal, and this implied some form of constitutional structure for society. Thoreau was right in protesting abuses by those in political power, but his civil disobedience was anarchical, and directed as much against the very idea of constituted authority as of abuses of power. Philosophically, Thoreau stood for independence from society rather than freedom in society. Thoreau carried out a one-man revolution. He was the apostle of independence, but not as a committed and loyal member of society, not as a citizen. Thoreau thought his relation to society was voluntaristic, rather than a matter of moral necessity. He made a classic case for individual independence against too many claims and demands on us by society and government.

But there is also a case for society against the anarchical claims of individuals who want to live *in* society but behave as though they lived *outside* society. The sweep to collectivism in our time abuses the case for society and leaves little room for individual liberty. Collectivism is a form of organized anarchy; its tyranny recognizes no constitutional restraints on power. Frost said he considered Thoreau's independence "an unchartered freedom." If each of us could live like a monk in a cell in the woods, and be content with a bean patch, Thoreau's social and economic theory would be sufficient. But it isn't enough for any man who isn't a saint, an ascetic, and a bachelor. Frost said he was none of these, and added: "Life among the woodchucks is not for me."

The idea of tyrannical restraints imposed on individuals from without led us to discuss censorship over writers. Frost told an amusing anecdote about how Kipling once sent a short story to a Christian Science magazine in which occurred the sentence: "She tossed off a glass of brandy." The editor knew many of his readers would be shocked by such unbecoming conduct by a member of the fair sex, so he wrote back and asked Kipling to change the sentence so that the word *brandy* would not appear in the story. Kipling was very obliging, and wrote back that he would delete the offensive word. When the manuscript was returned the sentence read: "She tossed off a glass of watermelons." That's the way to handle literary censorship, Frost said.

Frost launched on a related theme. He remarked that all social conflicts and evils in the world may be traced directly to two things which man possesses. The first of these is man's originality; the second is the strength of his conviction that his originality is true and should prevail. The strongest force in the world is our conviction about moral truth. Trouble in society begins when a man, such as Martin Luther, gets a new and original idea which no one has had in quite the same way before. He begins to talk about that idea until someone else gets it too. Then there are two of them. They begin talking about it to other people, and after a while each gets a convert. Then there are four of them. The process is continued until they become a party powerful enough to challenge the ruling authority. Since the ruling authority desires to stay in power the party is told it must get rid of that idea. But the people with the original idea say that since they believe in their idea they will not get rid of it, and if the ruling authority desires to get rid of the idea it must get rid of the people who believe in it. Often those in power are most reluctant to do this, as it would require harsh means, persecution, etc. If the rulers are smart they will incorporate the original idea, and declare the originator of it a saint, rather than excommunicate him as a heretic. That was what the Church did with St. Francis of Assisi. If those in authority cannot absorb the original idea they must destroy it, or they will be destroyed by it when enough people accept the original idea to overthrow their rulers. It is the same within nations and between nations. This is how wars begin. Originality is one of man's greatest virtues, and it keeps the gates of Utopia closed to man.

The right to hold original ideas is necessary for individual liberty. In a great and complex nation such as the United States individual originality often can become eccentricity, and eccentricity can become perverse and lead to madness. But under our system of government, Frost contended, we can absorb all that. The poet's strong nationalism came out in his defense of the many-faceted freedom throughout the United States.

One of the great freedoms he most enjoyed, Frost said, was to use the American language freely in his poetry. For most of the rest of our talk Frost explained his theory of the relationship between phonetics and semantics in poetry. He laid heavy stress upon "the sound of meaning and the meaning in sound." His theory of language was in some ways a subtle refinement of Wordsworth's theory that the natural idiom of common speech provides the basis for poetic diction. Unlike Wordsworth, Frost did not claim that peasants or semiliterate men provided the best source of diction for poetry. But he acknowledged that he had picked up many fine phrases from the motherwit idiom of New Hampshire and Vermont farmers. Among these he cited: "Good fences make good neighbors" (stressing the importance of *good*), in "Mending Wall"; "Sakes/It's only weather," in "The Runaway"; "Tell the truth for once," in "The Witch of Coos"; and "But just the kind that kinsfolk can't abide," in "The Death of the Hired Man." What made these common phrases poetry was the dramatic situation and tone in which they were spoken. Frost remarked that the most naturally dramatic language was gossip and that all literature is good to the extent that it is dramatic. John Synge understood this theory of language in poetry and applied the Irish vernacular and idiom with great skill in *The Playboy of the Western World*. Frost argued that every nation has its own idiom and a poet should not know too many foreign languages, because it dulls his sense of the idiomatic nuances of his own language. While writing a poem a poet is not a linguist but a creator.

Frost recalled that when he was in England, shortly before the First World War, he had pointed out to Walter De la Mare that the rhythm in portions of his poem "The Listeners" was remarkably loose for

English prosody. To illustrate what he meant by loose rhythm he quoted a passage from the poem:

> But only a host of phantom listeners
>   That dwelt in the lone house then
> Stood listening in the quiet of the moonlight
>   To that voice from the world of men:
> Stood thronging the faint moonbeams on the dark stair,
>   That goes down to the empty hall,
> Hearkening in an air stirred and shaken
>   By the lonely Traveller's call.

And one later line was a perfect example of loose rhythm: "Fell echoing through the shadowiness of the still house." The number of consecutive unstressed syllables in these lines was most unusual for English, Frost pointed out to De la Mare. But the English poet said he had never noticed anything unusual about these lines. Frost expressed his amazement over De la Mare's insensitivity to the phonetic patterns in his own poem.

I suggested that perhaps sensitivity to the sound of words was buried deep in the unconscious mind. Frost agreed, and said that in his sensitivity to the sound of words, before he understood their dictionary meaning, he "heard" every poem he wrote before putting it on paper. He could understand De la Mare's not being aware of the looseness of his rhythms in "The Listeners" while he was writing the poem, but he felt that afterwards De la Mare should have understood what he had achieved. Perhaps it was like not being aware of an unconscious pun we had made, I suggested. In poetry there were both conscious and unconscious puns. I said that Shakespeare was full of plays on words, conscious puns and deliberate double entendres. Frost agreed and added that Shakespeare's playing with words was a major source of his wit and humor, and made his poetry very rich in meaning. Multiple meanings in sound made for multiple meanings in the content. I asked whether a poet could ever be consciously aware of all the meanings in the sound or the content of his poems. Frost replied that he doubted that was possible. I then asked him whether he was aware of a pun in his poem "Mending Wall"? He looked startled. After a brief silence I quoted the lines with the pun:

> Before I built a wall I'd ask to know
> What I was walling in or walling out,
> And to whom I was like to give offense.

Frost howled with laughter, and shouted: "I'll take it! I'll take it! I'm entitled to every meaning to be found in my poem!" I admired his audacity in rising above the occasion, making valid humor out of what would have embarrassed a more timid man. A bit sheepishly he admitted that although he had said "Mending Wall" many times in public readings, he had been quite unaware of the pun. Perhaps, he added with a mischievous grin, De la Mare wasn't so insensitive after all. He completed his defense by saying: "Something there is that doesn't hear a pun." We laughed together over the whole thing. In stressing sound as the *vital* element in poetry, Frost said there was danger that the poet could fall into mere jingles if he made his meter too regular, without the grace and variety of rhythm. Tennyson, Swinburne, and Poe were often guilty of that error. I suggested adding Shelley to the list. Frost agreed, but with some qualification. Even in Shelley's "The Cloud" the sound of meaning saves it from becoming a jingle. Frost quoted the last stanza of "The Cloud" in a manner that roughened the too smooth beat of the meter. It wasn't Shelley at his best, Frost admitted. What was Shelley at his best? I asked. Frost quoted the final lines of "Ode to the West Wind":

> Drive my dead thoughts over the universe
> Like withered leaves to quicken a new birth!
> And, by the incantation of this verse,
>
> Scatter, as from an unextinguished hearth
> Ashes and sparks, my words among mankind!
> Be through my lips to unawakened earth
>
> The trumpet of a prophecy! O wind,
> If Winter comes, can Spring be far behind?

In these lines, said Frost, Shelley recognized that his earlier ideas were dead, unacceptable to mankind, and that he had been as Matthew Arnold was to describe him, "a beautiful but ineffectual angel beating in the void his luminous wings in vain." These lines were Shelley's hope or prophecy to himself that he would become a silent legislator to mankind by revitalizing his ideas and his art.

I asked Frost whether he agreed with Shelley's famous claim that poets are the silent legislators of mankind. He said that he did if the word *legislators* was not meant as anything like politicians who pass statutory laws. Poets are responsible for everything that touches the human spirit. Writing is the most powerful weapon for the dissemination of truth. The content of poetry consists of ideas that last. Artists are legislators more in the sense of Biblical prophets than of politicians, more like lawgivers than lawmakers.

We concluded our night together by quoting poems that we liked. Frost was pleased to learn that I knew four odes of Keats and some of his sonnets. Frost recited some English and Scottish ballads, and John Davidson's "A Ballad of Hell." Then with great verve he swung into Masefield's ballad, "Captain Stratton's Fancy" and, like a bard of old, chanted the quatrain that he deeply relished:

> Oh some that's good and godly ones they hold that it's a sin
> To troll the jolly bowl around and let the dollars spin;
> But I'm for toleration and for drinking at the inn,
> Says the old bold mate of Henry Morgan.

The beauty of the third line makes the whole poem live. Masefield disarms every reader by assuming that toleration and drinking at the inn were synonymous.

As we left the cabin Frost stopped at a table on the screened-in porch, scooped up a handful of acorns from a box, and dropped them into his pocket. It had rained for much of the previous night, and the earth along the side of the road was soft and still wet. We walked slowly, and from time to time Frost stopped, dug his heel into the earth, tossed an acorn into the crevice he had made, pressed it down into the soft spot, and covered it with his foot.

When we reached the road to Bread Loaf Frost kept on walking, with Gillie running ahead of us and back occasionally, and I asked Frost whether he was spoofing or serious in claiming that he as the poet was entitled to every "meaning" any reader could get out of his poems. Frost said he really believed he was entitled to every possible meaning. I asked, even if readers get nonsense? Frost said he was not responsible for their nonsense, for their poor reading comprehension.

Anything can be abused, including poetry. I asked, suppose two intelligent, sensitive readers, with good taste, get absolutely contradictory but plausible meanings from the same poem— doesn't one cancel out the other? Frost asked how one could be sure they are contradictory. What seems like a contradiction may only be a contrary that can be harmonized in a larger unity. In *Song of Myself,* Whitman says, "I am large, I contain multitudes." The immediate surface meaning in a poem often is enough for one reader, but not for another. It's better to leave a poem alone and read it without straining too hard after any so-called "hidden meaning." Frost cautioned, don't press poetry too far. Like everything in life, metaphors and symbols have a breaking point, and even good readers often don't show good judgment or taste in knowing when the breaking point in figures of speech has been reached. That is why readers can differ so markedly. But the poem is the same statement regardless of what any reader gets from it. And the same reader can get more out of a poem with a second or third reading, or when he has become more experienced with poetry. Does this constitute a contradiction? Or merely growth? Frost also stressed that it is not *what* the poem says that counts but *how* it says it. He quoted himself: "all the fun's in how you say a thing" (p. 44). The mood or tone is everything. The reader has to sense whether a line is coy, or ironical, or questioning, or asserting. The poet doesn't have any obligation to spell things out. Symbols and metaphors don't need to be explained.

And Robert Frost apparently felt he had explained his ideas about the "correspondence" between poet and reader sufficiently for this occasion, for suddenly he shook my hand, turned, and walked back down the road toward the Homer Noble farm. He could drop a conversation with the same sudden abruptness with which he could begin one.

III

The Bread Loaf School session was opened the following day, Friday, June 28, by President Moody, with Dean Harry Owen giving a fine talk on aesthetic theory and the "New Criticism." He paid a special tribute to John Crowe Ransom. On the following Monday evening, July 1, Frost gave his annual poetry reading to the assembled students, faculty, staff, summer resident guests, and visitors, in the Little Theatre.

Before and between reading his poems Frost made comments on the war in Europe and on American politics which were an almost verbatim repetition of what he had said at our two meetings in his cabin. I felt like someone who had attended a preview of a movie, or a dress rehearsal of a play, and was now witnessing its first public performance. He repeated his remark on how terrible it must be to cover the retreat of a beaten army, his comments in defense of Petain, and his strong conviction that the United States should stay out of the war until we had an important grievance against Germany. But Frost also added some observations to what he had said in the cabin. He was well aware that petitions were being circulated in many American colleges and universities urging the President and Congress to help Britain in every possible way short of going to war. Frost remarked that there were many "Anglophiles" eager to have the United States save Britain but that he was all for Britain saving herself. He did not admire Churchill for making obsequious overtures to the United States for help. There was a stir of protest among some members of his audience. One woman even spoke out loud her strong disagreement with what Frost said. Frost seemed to enjoy her opposition. The poet also expressed concern that President Roosevelt and the "New Deal bureaucrats" would use the war in Europe as an excuse for extending their domestic power over the American people. As long as we were at peace, he remarked, the war in Europe should loosen rather than tighten the controls of government at home. The war was lifting up the American economy, so that there were no longer plausible but fallacious economic arguments for retaining many of the existing regulations over agriculture, business, and industry. Frost was all for expanding freedom from politicians in each of these areas.

Frost read the usual favorites among his poems, "Mending Wall," "Birches," "Stopping by Woods on a Snowy Evening," but he also liked to mix in some of his lesser known and more recent poems. He read "A Drumlin Woodchuck," and then repeated the third stanza, emphasizing the lines

> As one who shrewdly pretends
> That he and the world are friends.

These lines, he said, apply to the United States and Japan. Perhaps we have more to fear from Japan than from Germany. Frost also read "Design" and remarked that in this sonnet he had reversed the Eighteenth-century argument from design, to prove the existence of God, by adding Darwin's theory of natural selection and the survival of the fittest. He read "Departmental," and commented ironically that this poem proved he was not a New England "regional poet," because his ant Jerry was a Florida ant. He read without comments "Provide, Provide," "Not Quite Social," "The Strong are Saying Nothing," and "Neither Out Far nor In Deep."

After Frost's poetry reading he and many people in the audience adjourned to the Bread Loaf Barn for refreshments and informal talk. The woman who had lost her temper and spoken out loud in protest during Frost's poetry reading approached him and berated him vehemently for not supporting Britain. She accused him of being anti-British. Frost was more amused than annoyed. It was ironical to Frost that having fought against Britain in our Revolution, and in the War of 1812, and over boundary disputes with Canada, and over many issues during the nineteenth century, including her anti-Union stand during the Civil War, we had fought on her side in 1917-18, and were now being pressured again to come to her defense. After the woman had lambasted Frost for awhile, he turned to her, and in a loud, mocking voice said: "Why, all those strong nations ought to be ashamed of themselves for picking on Germany." The woman almost collapsed with an apoplexy. Most of those around Frost could see he was spoofing her. Undoubtedly, she left Bread Loaf convinced that Frost was anti-British, when in fact he admired much about the British and simply wanted them to show their best character in the war, without American participation in it. When war came to America with Pearl Harbor he gave up bantering those who seemed to him to hold extreme views, out of harmony with the real self-interest of America.

IV

A week after Frost's poetry reading Harry Owen told me he had arranged with Frost for the two of them to have a private lunch with me at Bread Loaf, to celebrate my having received the Elinor Frost Fellowship. On Wednesday, July 10, I was relieved of waiting table for that day, the chef at Bread Loaf, Eddie Doucette, baked a cake for the occasion, and Frost, Owen, and I enjoyed lunch together in the dining room, sitting at a table along "Fingerbowl Alley" with the paying guests. Owen had bought from the Bread Loaf Bookstore a copy of the new printing of the *Collected Poems of Robert Frost* (Halcyon House Edition, 1939), and at the lunch Frost inscribed the book: "Robert Frost to Peter Stanlis, Bread Loaf, 1940." Next to my name he made an asterisk, and below his inscription he wrote: "For very special reason." As he handed the book to me Frost said: "People will ask you what was the very special reason, and then you can tell them about your fellowship." It was clear that Robert Frost understood the importance of a good public press. Over the years his prediction proved true.

After my lunch with Frost and Owen, the poet returned to the campus that evening to attend John Crowe Ransom's poetry reading from his book *Chills and Fever.* Ransom read his poems without comments, in a soft, Southern accent, with just a touch of primness to add an element to his irony. Afterward, Frost commented very favorably on Ransom's poetry. During the school session Frost visited the campus from time to time, most often to play tennis with Kay Morrison or another friend. Once he had dinner at the Inn as the guest of Lee Simonson, the Director of the New York Theatre Guild, whom Frost admired. Simonson had visited Frost in Ripton the year before. Later in July Frost attended a talk by Edward Weeks, editor of the *Atlantic Monthly,* of whom he thought very well.

On July 27 Frost came to the campus in the morning to hear "The Vermont Balladeers" sing old ballads of Vermont. These singers were sponsored by Helen Hartness Flanders, wife of the United States senator from Vermont, and they were invited to Bread Loaf by Donald Davidson, whose passion for old ballads was as strong as that of Frost. Among the ballad singers was Edward "Grandpa" Dragon, the head of the numerous Dragon clan in Ripton, famous throughout central Vermont for his ballad singing, square dancing, and hard drinking. He was in his eighties and was reputed able to outsing, outdance, outdrink, and outdo everyone else in everything in all Vermont. Frost admired him very much. At our lunch together, Harry Owen told Frost and me an anecdote about "Grandpa" Dragon which tickled us. Some students at Dartmouth College had invited "Grandpa" Dragon to sing his ballads at a student assembly at Dartmouth. He arrived several hours before he "was scheduled to perform, and the students had plied him with liquor, so that he was well-lubricated when he stepped up to the platform. The ballad singing had been advertised as a cultural event, and many dignified matrons and culture vultures were in the audience. "Grandpa" Dragon proceeded to sing some of his bawdiest ballads, to the vast delight of the students and the embarrassed chagrin of the matrons. At Bread Loaf "Grandpa" Dragon was cold sober, and his spontaneous singing charmed everyone. He even made some comments about how the ballads were composed, saying that in the cold Vermont winters, when the mountain folks were snowed in, as they wove baskets they also wove ballads to warm their hearts.

V

On July 29 Sir Wilfred Grenfell spoke at noon to the Bread Loaf School on his work among the poor in Labrador and was very enthusiastically received. That evening Allen Tate, who had come to Bread Loaf to visit John Crowe Ransom, lectured in the Little Theatre on the poetry of John Donne and John Keats and was coolly received. Tate began his lecture by saying that if anyone were to ask where did the Nashville Fugitives come from, no one could answer, but if anyone were to ask whither have they flown, the answer would be "to Bread Loaf." Tate's lecture was centered in a comparison of the techniques of Donne and Keats in introducing and developing images and metaphors in their poetry, in order to convey meaning.

Tate noted that in Donne's lyric, "Go and catch a falling star," the first stanza consisted of a series of seven images, inductively and imperatively ordered, as commands to do impossible things. In the second and third stanzas these imperative impossibilities were applied functionally through two conditional suppositions, to advance the theme. Or as the "New Critics" would put it, the first stanza was the "vehicle" for the "tenor" in the last two stanzas. The "texture" of the detailed images in the first stanza, complicated by the tone of sustained irony, combined to create the "structure" of each stanza and to provide unity and logical coherence throughout the poem. Donne's lyric was unified in structure, logic, tone, imagery, and theme, and therefore it was an excellent poem. Tate then analyzed Donne's "A Valediction Forbidding Mourning" and showed how the same requisite unity was achieved deductively through Donne's famous extended metaphor comparing two lovers to the two arms of a mariner's compass. In contrast to Donne's two poems Tate cited the opening quatrain of Keats's "Ode to a Grecian Urn" and pointed out that each image was made and then broken, without forming a part of any logical induction leading to a later conclusion and without any logical extension of any one image. Only the loosest kind of association existed between the images, and consequently the theme was left very ambiguous. For these reasons and others, Tate concluded, since these characteristics generally prevailed in the poetry of Donne and Keats, Donne was a more unified and better poet than Keats.

Several days after Tate's lecture, I visited Frost at his cabin and summarized at his request the argument, examples, and thesis advanced by Tate. Frost listened with great attention, then remarked that the lecture showed that Tate preferred Donne to Keats, but it didn't prove that Donne was a superior poet to Keats. Donne might be superior in strict logic, but inferior in suggestive connotations in meaning. But logic was only one of several possible principles of arrangement by which to lay out images and metaphors in poetry. The relationship between figures of speech in a poem might be logical, or analogical, or psychological, or grammatical, or associative, or emotional, or tonal—the last being of greatest importance for unity. Tate preferred the inductive and deductive logic of Donne to the psychological, associative, emotional, and tonal techniques of Keats, because a logical arrangement lends itself better to the analytical methods of the new critics. But there are many good poems in which sense is conveyed through sound and other non-logical techniques, as well as or better than it could be through strict logic. It is weak reasoning, Frost concluded with an ironical grin, to make reason and logic the supreme criteria for unity in a poem, and weaker still to generalize as Tate had done. Frost added that he thought Tate was a better poet than he was a critic and wished he would write more poetry and less criticism.

I mentioned to Frost that the next day (August 1) Ransom and Theodore Meyer Greene (Princeton University) were lecturing jointly on I. A. Richards's *Principles of Literary Criticism,* to be followed the next night by Philip Wheelwright (Dartmouth College), lecturing on "The Assertion of Truth in Poetry." There would be open discussions after each lecture. I stated that during much of the summer session Ransom had praised Wheelwright highly for illuminating the relationship between linguistic symbols and semantics in poetry. In his

"Analysis of Poetry" course Ransom was much concerned with how "meaning" is conveyed in a poem and with the relationship between "belief" and "truth" in poetry.

Frost shook his head sadly. He said he knew all these men and had talked recently with Greene and several times during the summer with Ransom. Both of them, as well as Wheelwright, were paying too much attention to I. A. Richards. The trouble with Richards, Frost said, was that he believed language and psychology were exact sciences and that therefore critical theory could provide a rational and scientific foundation for the practical criticism of poetry and all imaginative literature. Ransom's "New Criticism" was moving dangerously close to that position. It didn't matter that Richards distinguished between how language was used by scientists in its literal sense and how it was used figuratively by poets. Richards's whole object was to make language, however used, as scientific as possible. Frost denied categorically that the methods of appreciating and understanding poetry could be made into an experimental, theoretical, or practical exact science. Ever since the seventeenth century the Western world had moved from applying the methods of science to physical nature, or matter, to what has come to be called "social science" and "political science." These terms are misnomers, and create false hopes and delusions, because society and politics cannot be understood with anything like the exactness with which atoms, molecules, and matter in general can be understood. There are still mysteries about what matter is and probably always will be. Richards and others wanted to extend the methods of science beyond the physical and social to include poetry and imaginative literature. Some of these men recognized a qualitative difference between physical nature and human nature, and the extent to which values are human in origin, so they would be shocked by the accusation that they were trying to do to literature what Watson and Pavlov and other sociological behaviorists were trying to do to men in society. Nevertheless, that was what they were attempting to do, and they were doomed to fail. It couldn't work. Frost had become somewhat heated as he talked, and at this point he drew himself upright in his Morris chair, shook his pointed index finger vehemently, and almost shouted: "The twentieth century will be remembered in history for having finally determined the true role of science in human affairs." He concluded by prophesying that men will find that science will fall far short of exact, absolute, predictable knowledge, especially as applied to men.

I asked Frost to explain further why he objected to the term "political science." He said he agreed with Aristotle that politics was a branch of ethics and that ethical principles and values were God-given or man-made, and could not be determined by scientific methods. Politics was concerned with what was "good" for men in their memberships, in society, and not with what was "true" in theory. A political philosophy was best tested by its practical consequences to men in society. Frost objected to speculative theory so far as it reversed the relationship between truth as theory and good in practice, and made men indifferent to the practical consequences of their supposed "truths." Frost put the question to me: "How else can anyone explain Stalin's willingness to 'liquidate' (dread word) millions of Russian farmers in order to establish their collective farms?"

Frost said that from very early life he had rejected any form of radical socialism. He recalled his childhood in California: "In my boyhood I read the radical works of Edward Bellamy and Henry George, but I have never been a radical." He remarked that upon reading George's socialism he rejected it immediately, "because like all socialism it is bad arithmetic, in which two comes before one." Frost said he never believed that politics based upon compulsory social benevolence was superior to politics based upon freedom to pursue legitimate self-interest.

I told Frost I was puzzled, because if science is so important in the twentieth century I wondered why he had not more often used science as a subject for his poetry. Frost replied: "Read my book." Later when I went back to his poetry, I was surprised to discover how many poems dealt with astronomy and botany.

As an example of how scientists revised their claims about knowledge, Frost remarked that scientists used to say the speed of light was absolute but now say light travels faster than they had believed. Geologists are constantly pushing the supposed age of the earth back farther and farther in time. Frost said he had once had a conversation with Niels Bohr, the famous Danish physicist, who had told him what he wanted most to know about atoms passing through a screen. Bohr had said that scientists could predict how many atoms would pass through, but they could not say which ones would pass through. Frost remarked that from this fact we could understand why scientists dealt with statistical averages, and could not say how any individual human being would respond to their experiments. Bohr had confirmed Frost's skepticism about the claims of social scientists that their methods were exact and their results predictable.

VI

Early in August Frost again came to the campus on the invitation of Professor Lucia Mirrielees, to speak to her students, all of whom were high school English teachers, on how to teach writing and literature in high school. He was full of bantering good humor yet deadly serious in the arguments he advanced. He began by claiming to be the greatest expert on American education from having run away from as much of it as he could. He observed the ironical paradox that American public school education was "free and compulsory," that no one was free to stay away from it until he was sixteen years old. He said the greatest failure of American education in teaching fundamentals of knowledge and skill was in our high schools; the greatest failure in teaching students how to think for themselves, instead of going around and repeating what others have said, was in our colleges; the greatest failure to treat the liberal arts humanistically, rather than scientifically, was in our graduate schools. At this point Frost noticed the students all had their notebooks out and were writing furiously. He paused and waited until everyone was looking up, then asked: "Do you know the difference between a student in high school and a student in college? When a high school teacher greets her class 'Good morning,' everyone answers, 'Good morning.' But when a college professor says 'Good morning,' everyone writes it in a notebook." Everyone laughed a bit sheepishly. Some students put their pens away and listened.

Frost admitted that our own best original thoughts often deserved to be recorded, but not someone else's commonplaces on public knowledge delivered in a lecture. He told an anecdote about how his daughter once heard him say that keeping a notebook on a teacher's lectures was a foolish waste of time. When she went to college she was told by her English professor that she had to keep a notebook, and she refused. Her professor became incensed at this insubordination and called her aside one day after class and told her she was setting a bad example for the rest of the class. Frost's daughter said she thought she was setting a good example, but since the teacher thought otherwise she would leave the class. The professor happened to know Frost and feared the poet would be displeased, and being a bit embarrassed over how things stood he called Frost's daughter up and told her she could attend his class without keeping a notebook. Then he hastened to add: "But of course I can't give you an A!" Frost laughed uproariously at his punch line.

Frost's anecdote was a good example of what he meant by a teacher's addiction to foolish required assignments and the binding force of academic machinery. He told of how after he had read his poems at a New England girls' college a student came bubbling up to him and said: "Just think, Mr. Frost, you are required reading in my poetry course!" Frost was not happy to be thus flattered, and replied: "Just think what happened to Longfellow from being required reading!" One of the troubles with institutional education at every level is that teachers feel they must measure a student's performance, and therefore they are primarily testers and graders. Frost admitted that there was probably no way for schools to avoid giving grades, and he would certainly rather give a letter grade to a student than use adjectives on him. But in high school, English teachers could at least avoid assignments of mere busy work in getting factual knowledge and give assignments which truly draw out the intellectual and literary ability of a student. A teacher could ask a student: "Can you recall any simile or metaphor which you made recently which you thought was especially good at the time you made it?" Grade your students on that, he said. Base the final grade for a course on the best original idea, image, metaphor, or analogy the student makes during the course. In high school, students should learn to take wing and soar, instead of which they learn to hate education and poetry by being weighed down with useless heavy requirements. High school is the creative period of a student's life; there will be time enough for him to become critical and scholarly in college. Never ask high school students to be too scientifically exact and thorough; let them disport themselves in playing with ideas and metaphors. Only then will we help young students to grow into writers, and make our literature match our national wealth.

Frost poked hilarious fun at Mortimer Adler's recently published book, *How to Read a Book,* saying that if a student doesn't know how to read he will not know how to read *How to Read a Book,* and if he does know how to read he doesn't need Adler's book. No one acquires a sound taste and critical understanding of literature by a technique or gimmick. Understanding takes place automatically when students experience life and literature together. As we grow older, the more and better we read poetry the more things we can do better with other poems we read. If a student doesn't understand how poetry works, he won't get a poem by having it analyzed for him. But most children naturally love stories and songs and sense the parables in them, from fairy tales and ballads to the most profound fiction and poetry we have. It's all the same thing, saying one thing in terms of another, being playful about the common verities.

So much for education, Frost said. He paused to see if anyone had any questions. A student wondered how it would be possible to enforce class discipline if assignments were not strictly required. Frost replied that of course certain assignments had to be required, as when a class read a play together to act out some scenes. But many assignments could be open invitations for students to perform or write whenever they could. Discipline problems were the result of enforced attendance at school and boredom. Frost told a story of how after he quit Dartmouth College, and took over his mother's school in Methuen, Massachusetts, he had to physically discipline with a cane a group of rowdy students who constantly disrupted his class. The leader of these rowdies was a half-breed Indian named Johnny Howe. The chairman of the Methuen School Board was all for expelling Howe, but Frost insisted he could handle Johnny, and Howe continued in school until after Frost himself quit teaching. Years later Frost was passing through Methuen and visited the former chairman of the school board, long retired. While discussing the past Frost asked: "Whatever became of Johnny Howe?" The former chairman of the school board replied: "Why, Johnny's one of our most esteemed citizens. He's currently chairman of the school board!" After the loud laughter had died, Frost remarked: "Neither in religion nor in education should we shut the gates of salvation on anyone."

On the art of teaching poetry in high school, Frost repeated much that he had said in 1939, but he added some new thoughts. He expressed considerable doubt that poetry could be "taught" through organized education. Perhaps the best a teacher can do is to show by example how much poetry means to him. Show enthusiasm for ideas, metaphors, and the forms of poetry, and hope it rubs off as enthusiasm in the students. Enthusiasm can be crude or very refined, and it is best developed in a sense of play, as on the athletic field. If teachers can make the reading of poetry as much a game as sports, they will teach their students to love poetry, and in time the students will acquire taste and judgment, and will know when metaphor and analogies are fresh and valid and when they are not. Only then will they be educated in poetry.

In teaching writing in high school, Frost wondered, beyond correctness in mechanics what can a teacher hope to do? It is hard enough to pump out mistakes in grammar and logic without also hoping to turn out polished writers. Frost doubted that anyone could "teach" someone how to write a good poem. He threw off an aphorism: "A poem should be at least as good as the prose it might have been." Otherwise stick to prose. Begin with tossing ideas around, and hope it will end in a student's taking fire and throwing off sparks of metaphors. That is a world above having students be parrots or busy work drones. If a person can't think for himself he is better off not saying anything. Then at least he bores or annoys only himself. In teaching how to write good prose, beyond mechanical correctness, teachers can show a student how to back up an abstract statement with a concrete image. For instance, if a student should write, "She clinched the effect," he could add to it, "She stuck its tail down its throat." But above all give the students lots of leisure to write. And if they don't write, or if they fail in writing, what does it matter? Writing, and especially poetry, is the easiest kind of art in which to fail. But mercifully for those who fail—or even for those who would not have failed if they had persisted and had the will and courage to see it through to their maximum talent (and these are the commonest failures in writing) — writing is also the easiest art to slip out of unnoticed. You can leave by the back door and no one will say a word.

VII

The Writers' Conference of 1940 was in many ways a repetition of the patterns established by the various clinics and events in 1939, but with some new staff members, and a totally new body of conferees. Again Frost appeared to be in his true element, far more than at the

School of English. He thoroughly enjoyed seeing such old friends as Herschel Brickell, Raymond Everitt, John Gassner, Edith Mirrielees, Fletcher Pratt, and Louis Untermeyer. But this summer "Benny" DeVoto was absent from the staff, and his place in the fiction clinics was taken by John P. Marquand and Wallace Stegner, both of whom had attended the Writers' Conference in 1939 as speakers. They had been so impressive in their comments on fiction that they were invited back for the entire session in 1940. Frost thought that Marquand and Stegner were outstanding fiction writers, although he esteemed Ernest Hemingway as perhaps the best American novelist. Of Hemingway, Frost said: "He's a great one." One of the most pleasant tasks Harry Owen ever assigned to me at Bread Loaf was to go to Middlebury in the taxi to meet John P. Marquand, to escort him to the campus, and see that he was comfortably settled in Maple Cottage. Owen's attention to such minute details was in part what made him such a fine administrator of Bread Loaf. I had read and admired Marquand's novel, *The Late George P. Apley,* and enjoyed talking a bit about it with the author. The twelve-mile drive from Middlebury to Bread Loaf, spent discussing fiction with Marquand, was one of my most delightful literary experiences during the six years I attended the Writers' Conference.

Marquand was an elegantly cool, sophisticated, dignified, pipe-smoking, quiet-spoken gentleman, with a neat trimmed mustache. He was as impeccably dressed and debonair as one of his suave fictional socialite Bostonians. Yet he was a friendly and accessible man, and enjoyed talking literary shop. In many ways he was the antithesis of Frost, and differed even more from his young Western colleague, Wallace Stegner, yet all three writers had a profound respect for one another's work, and got along well at Bread Loaf. I enjoyed Marquand's talk so much that on two occasions when Frost did not attend the poetry clinics I sat in on the fiction clinics to hear Marquand.

Edith Mirrielees ran the fiction clinics, and she was a most competent and perceptive critic of fiction, especially strong in technique and form. On one occasion she read a short story by a conferee, and everyone sensed that although it was an interesting story, centered in a common and inherently dramatic human problem, something was subtly and radically wrong with it. Miss Mirrielees prodded the conferees to identify the problem and suggest methods of solving it.

A few tried but floundered. Stegner suggested that a change in the point of view, from omniscient author to a participant narrator, would improve it. Everyone agreed on that. Miss Mirrielees suggested that some concrete details in the setting, plot action, and characterizations would improve the story. Everyone agreed with that. Marquand had remained silent throughout the discussion. Finally, Miss Mirrielees turned to him. In a quiet and casual manner he showed how by violating the purely chronological arrangement of the plot, and transposing the episodes so that the reader was plunged into the climactic action at the beginning, through a series of flashbacks gradually leading back to the central conflict, the short story could be redeemed. He noted that an epic structure in miniature was far more dramatic than chronological expository narration. He concluded by urging that much of the description be changed to dialogue. When Marquand had finished there was a sustained moment of complete silence, followed by enthusiastic applause. Everyone knew that his diagnosis and recommendations were absolutely letter right.

Two other newcomers on the staff were Walter Pritchard Eaton (Yale University), in drama, and Barbara Fleury, from Michigan, in children's literature. I had played some hot games of croquet on the West Lawn with Eaton during his visit to the Writers' Conference in 1939, and this summer we resumed our friendly rivalry and played croquet every day through the Conference. Eaton was a tall, thin, wiry man, a salty New England old timer, with a keen wit that reminded me of Frost. He and Frost enjoyed talking together.

Barbara Fleury was a very attractive young woman, to whom Frost took an immediate liking because of their many friends in common at the University of Michigan. On one occasion, before the scheduled clinics began, Frost and Miss Fleury stood outside the Little Theatre talking, and Frost introduced me to her, so she could tell me about the extensive creative writing program at Michigan. She and Frost told me about the annual Hopwood Awards in writing at Michigan, the largest money prizes for students in the United States. Miss Fleury had taken writing courses with Professor Roy W. Cowden and others at Ann Arbor, and she had won a major Hopwood Award in fiction and had gone on to success in writing books for children. Frost and Miss Fleury also talked about other people they knew at Michigan, professors Clarence De Witt Thorpe and Louis I. Bredvold, and Dean

Joseph A. Bursley, and Mary Cooley, whom Miss Fleury said ran the
Hopwood Room. Frost said that she was one of the original "three
graces" who printed the literary magazine the *Whimsies,* when he
was at Michigan as poet in residence in the early 1920s. Frost remarked
that among large American universities he knew of only two—Michigan
and Iowa—which paid much attention to original writing. In addition to
its fine writing program the University of Michigan had one of the best
departments of English in the nation. It was most unusual to hear Frost
speak so warmly about any academic institution. Michigan, as Frost and
Barbara Fleury described it, sounded like a school that combined the two
things that interested me most—a sound academic program and creative
writing. But in the summer of 1940 I had no way of knowing that this
conversation, plus others with Frost about Michigan over the next four
summers, would send me to Ann Arbor in the fall of 1944.

Early during the Writers' Conference Frost gave a poetry reading, but because I was in Middlebury on an errand for Harry Owen
I missed it. I heard afterwards that he spoke on writing poetry as a
craft. Frost and Untermeyer again combined to run the poetry clinics.
No unusual incidents occurred at the clinics, and the poems submitted
by the conferees were better in general than those discussed in 1939.
Indeed the whole Conference ran very smoothly, under the humane
administration of Ted Morrison, and the clinics, lectures, literary talk,
square dances, softball games, tennis matches, and parties at Treman
Cottage and the Barn filled the days and nights of everyone at Bread
Loaf with pleasant and stimulating activities.

Two memorable speakers were at Bread Loaf that summer, W. H.
Auden and Katherine Anne Porter. Auden was a very shy and self-
conscious man, most difficult to engage in conversation. But when
he stepped up to the podium to give his poetry reading he seemed to
catch fire. He brought no book, but quoted his poems from memory in
a rapid-fire, nonstop manner, which made it difficult for his audience
to absorb what he said. Also, he distracted his listeners by his awkward
way of standing at the podium. He lifted one leg almost halfway up
the podium, and stood on the other leg and leaned heavily over the
podium while he recited a poem. Between poems he would sometimes
change legs. About half way through Auden's performance a thunder-
storm struck. The Bread Loaf Little Theatre has no partition between
the roof and the hall, to absorb sound, and giant hailstones rained an

incessant tattoo on the roof, so that no one could hear Auden beyond the first several rows of seats. After a while the podium was moved to the side of the hall, next to the fireplace, and chairs were swung around in a close semicircle. But it was still impossible to hear well, and as the storm continued Auden finally quit reciting his poems. After the storm subsided everyone adjourned to the Barn, where Auden and Carson McCullers huddled together in a corner and talked and sipped their drinks and ignored everyone. Like Auden, McCullers was very shy and introvertive. In her sailor boy's shirt and her hair in bangs she looked like a nineteen-year-old pixie.

Katherine Anne Porter read a brief short story and spoke very sensibly through it on the techniques and art of the short story. She confirmed the theory and practice of writing fiction so richly set forth in the fiction clinics by Miss Mirrielees and Wallace Stegner. During a brief question period following her talk, Eudora Welty engaged her in a pleasant but searching dialogue on several points. When the meeting broke up they converged, and as they drifted off with the rest of the staff to Treman Cottage they continued to talk. The visual image of these two ladies talking about fiction, while oblivious to everyone around them, is almost archetypal.

One of the most entertaining events at the Writers' Conference was Louis Untermeyer's performance as master of revels in a program he organized called "Information Tease," a literary parody of the popular radio show "Information Please." Untermeyer fielded written questions from the conferees, identifications of passages of poetry, obscure facts about author's lives and works, etc., to a panel consisting of Ted Morrison, Fletcher Pratt, and Walter Pritchard Eaton. Every question he read, every answer or nonanswer he received, provoked what appeared to be a spontaneous and outrageous pun. Never was Untermeyer more "the punning pundit of Bread Loaf." Finally, he read a question directed to him: "Which literary man among Bread Loafers was infamous as a punster?" Untermeyer looked blank and professed to be totally baffled by the question. Why was *he* asked to answer it? "Once apun a time, perhaps on opunning night," he might have known the answer, but "upun my word" it was too much for him now. His clowning was clever and lightly amusing, and probably relieved the tension of some nervous conferees. Later, everyone adjourned to the Barn, and

Untermeyer conducted a barber-shop sextet of staff and fellows singing summer camp songs. In the choruses of several songs the booming bass voice of John Ciardi lingered on after everyone else's had run out of breath.

On the last day of the Conference I said goodbye to Frost and expressed the hope that I would be back next summer. He suggested that if I should come to Boston before he left for Florida in January I should visit him. He gave me his address and phone number. With that we parted, and several days later I returned to Middlebury, contented with having enjoyed the most stimulating and profitable summer of my life.

VIII

After spending Christmas vacation with my family in Nutley, New Jersey, on December 29, 1940, I went to Hyde Park, Massachusetts, to visit a Middlebury College friend, Robert Burnes. We planned to attend a New Year's Eve party in Boston with friends before returning to Middlebury. On New Year's Eve, shortly before we were to leave we received word that our host had been rushed to the hospital with pneumonia, so the party was cancelled. I proposed that we telephone Robert Frost to see if he would like us to stop by for a visit. By luck Frost was at home alone and said he would be glad to see us.

We arrived at Frost's apartment around 10 P.M. He lived at 88 Mt. Vernon Street, just off Louisburg Square in Boston. As he greeted us I made a joke in introducing my college friend: "Robert Frost, meet your fellow Scotch poet, Robert Burnes." Bob laughed and admitted to being Scottish but said he was an economics major whose family expected him to go into the family business of selling furniture. We settled down for an evening of good talk.

Frost commented that the idolatry and love the Scottish people have for Robert Burns is incredible. Although the Scots respected James Thomson, and had put up a statue of Allan Ramsay in Edinburgh, and remembered Robert Blair and James Macpherson, among Scottish poets Robert Burns was king. Frost remarked that the Scots quoted Burns everywhere and that celebrations of his birthday in Scotland and in the United States and Canada have been known to last much longer than celebrations of Shakespeare's birthday among the English. I suggested that perhaps the Scots were celebrating

Burns's well-known prowess with the ladies. They laughed, and Frost acknowledged that Bobby Burns was certainly filled to overflowing with Romantic sensibility about women. Frost then punned that in the end Burns's "amour was all for Jean Armour." But except for a few really fine poems, such as "The Cotter's Saturday Night" and "To a Mouse," I wondered whether Burns was really as good a poet as many literary critics thought. This heretical remark was politely ignored. Frost said how wonderful it was for Burns's memory that within two hours everyone in the English speaking world would be singing "Auld Lang Syne." That shut me up.

Frost contended that Burns was unique to the Scottish people because in his poetry he so obviously liked everything about his country's past, its language, its songs and stories, its heroes, such as Robert and Bruce Douglas, its people's clannishness and patriotism— everything that made the Scots proud of themselves as a people. Burns's popularity was a sign that the people were returning his love with theirs. Frost recalled that once as a schoolboy in Lawrence, Massachusetts, he had watched his English teacher put on the board some stanzas of William Collins's poem "How Sleep the Brave," which celebrated the heroism of the Scottish soldiers killed in the battle of Culloden Moor. It had made him realize how close poetry could be to the crucial events of life. I remarked on the irony of that battle and poem, that the Highland Scots army of "Bonnie Prince Charlie," Pretender to the throne of Great Britain, was defeated by a combination of Lowland Scots and English. Frost said that religion as well as politics sometimes made strange bedfellows, but if the Stuarts wouldn't be Protestants they couldn't hope to rule in Britain.

Frost recalled that when he and his family had sailed from Boston to Glasgow in 1912, with his first sight of the Hebrides and the shore of Scotland he experienced the special thrill of something like a homecoming. When he had seen battleships at anchor he had made the mistake of referring to "the English navy" in the presence of a Scottish sailor, who corrected him: it was "the British navy." This conscious sense of their nationalism was one of the things that made the Scots among the most energetic and intelligent race the world has ever known. Geography, religion, and nationalism were the chief sources of their strength. I could feel my friend Bob Burnes glowing with pride as Frost spoke.

Frost proceeded to review the contributions which various races had made toward the development of civilization from the dawn of historical time to the present. The yellow race had created a pretty respectable civilization and culture in ancient times, in its laws, customs, and art, but the Chinese and Japanese were hampered by a cumbersome written language, were limited in science and had leveled out several centuries ago. The same was true of the brown races of the Pacific islands, India, and the Near East. India and Egypt had shown their high water marks in creating civilization. In Africa the Negro races had achieved even less in literature and science. Perhaps the tropical climate was a factor in determining where they had leveled off. But what a race the white has been! Its cultural achievements in the arts—witness the Greeks—and in law, government and literature—witness the Romans, British, and French —and its intellectual achievements in science—witness Germany, the United States and all Europe—have increased man's hold on the planet beyond what any other races have contributed. Among the most intelligent and energetic of the white race were the Jews and the Scots. Though few in number they had contributed mightily to improve civilization and culture in Europe and America. Bob Burnes remarked that like any impartial and modest Scot he couldn't argue much with that!

We talked and sipped drinks until midnight, then touched glasses and toasted one another with good wishes for a happy new year. While Bob Burnes was in the bathroom Frost asked me in a very quiet voice whether I had heard that his son Carol had committed suicide in October. I told him that Harry Owen had informed me of this tragedy, and I expressed my sympathy. I had seen Carol Frost only once, very briefly during a visit one day to the Homer Noble farm last summer. As I went up to the cabin past the barn I had passed a rather strange and morbid looking man, but had not spoken to him nor he to me. Frost remarked that he had seen his son's tragedy coming on over a long time and had tried to head it off, but that he had failed in this as in so many other things in his family. But he was now determined not to allow this latest failure to get him down. His grandson Prescott had shown him what true courage was, and in this new year he would raise himself up again, as he had done after his wife died. I was deeply moved and very pleased by Frost's words. He was not a man to wear his sorrows on his sleeve. Yet privately he was realistic and courageous in facing the shattering sorrows of his domestic tragedies. I acquired renewed respect and affection for him for that.

Frost inquired about friends and events in Middlebury. I told him that Harry Owen and "Doc" Cook were both well and nourishing, as was President Moody, but that his old friend Vernon Harrington was not at all well. I informed him that a new student literary magazine had been started, called *Directions,* in which I had published an essay on William Blake. Frost said he was interested in student publications, and I promised to send him a copy soon.

We got into a discussion of poetry, and Bob Burnes remarked that he particularly liked Frost's "Stopping by Woods on a Snowy Evening," especially the last stanza. Frost expressed the hope that unlike some readers Burnes did not read the line "But I have promises to keep" to mean unpleasant "promises," duties and practical obligations to others. Frost objected that such an interpretation was too narrow. The "promises" could also be about longstanding ambitions to be fulfilled by the speaker, or other hopes and desires. Frost remarked that there was danger of reading too much into poetry through being too specific while leaving out part of what was there. He acknowledged that William Empson had a valid point about the seven types of ambiguity to be found in poetry, although he did not know why ambiguity should be limited to the magic number seven. Poetry is filled with ambiguities. Some words and phrases are most unfortunate in connotation. As an example, he asked whether we had ever noticed the line in Coleridge's "Kubla Khan," "As if this earth in fast thick pants were breathing." (Even in Coleridge's day "pants" was short for "pantaloons," or men's trousers.) I didn't quite know what to make of Frost's comment, but it appeared to be a preliminary statement to a distinction in dramatic monologues: the contrast was between "rhetorical passages" and "speaking passages," images and metaphors which tended to be descriptive: quick thoughts and direct actions which captured the tone and posture of the speaking voice so completely that in a poem each character could be recognized without the author's identification.

Frost's remarks reminded Bob Burnes and me of a friend of ours at Middlebury, my classmate Douglas H. Mendel, Jr., who performed dramatic monologues of poems and one-act plays in which he alone did all the parts. He had spent the past summer at a large resort hotel

Dear Stanlis:
You sent me a good readable magazine. I like its looks too. My only suggestion is that your quotations shouldn't be altogether from reviews of books. (The quotations are quite an idea.) Your own essay on Blake smacks a little too much of essay in the sense of effort It is a hard kind of thing to write at your age. But it is the kind of thing there is the largest lack of and greatest opening for in American letters at this time.

We haven't anyone alive but the soda pop over night critic of the current book of the month. I should think someone could make a modest living and a good position with deliberate criticism of past and present literature blended in the proportion of say two or three to one. You are still too fresh from the classroom. But you make a beginning in the kind of career I wish more of for my country.

Remember me to my friends.

Ever yours
Robert Frost

88 Mt Vernon St Boston Mass
June 1941

in the Catskill Mountains earning money by entertaining vacation-
ers with his monologues. His repertoire included Browning's "My
Last Duchess" and "Andrea del Sarto," and Frost's "Mending Wall,"
"Home Burial," and "The Death of the Hired Man," the last being
the most popular monologue. He had also performed these poems
in November at a meeting of the Middlebury College Literary Club.
Frost was delighted with our account of how Doug Mendel managed
to vary the voices of each character without having to identify the
speaker. It confirmed his theory that truly dramatic poetry conveys
meaning through sounds.

Bob Burnes and I stayed with Frost until around 1:30 A.M. As we
were leaving he gave each of us a copy of a little book, *From Snow
to Snow* (New York: Henry Holt and Co., 1936), consisting of Frost's
selections of his most appropriate poem for each month through the
calendar year. He inscribed in mine: "To Peter Stanlis from his friend
Robert Frost Christmas 1940 Boston." He also inscribed Bob Burnes's
copy, and gave me another inscribed copy for Doug Mendel. He said
he was leaving for Florida in two weeks, so I promised to send him a
copy of *Directions* as soon as I returned to Middlebury.

Ten days after I sent Frost our college literary magazine, on January
14, 1941, I received from the poet a letter commenting on it:

Dear Stanlis:
You sent me a good readable magazine. I like its looks too. My only suggestion is that your quotations shouldn't be altogether from reviews of books.
(The quotations are quite an idea.) Your own essay on Blake smacks a little too
much of essay in the sense of effort. It is a hard kind of thing to write at your
age. But it is the kind of thing there is the largest lack of and greatest opening
for in American letters at this time. We haven't anyone alive but the soda pop
overnight critic of the current book of the month. I should think someone could
make a modest living and a good position with deliberate criticism of past and
present literature blended in the proportion of say two or three to one. You are
still too fresh from the classroom. But you make a beginning in the kind of career
I wish more of for my country. Remember me to my friends.
Ever yours
Robert Frost
88 Mt. Vernon St Boston Mass Jan 11 1941

This was to be my last contact with Frost until late in June, just
before the opening of the 1941 Bread Loaf School session.

Robert Frost at Bread Loaf: 1941

I

During the spring of 1941, to make room for the anticipated student enrollment, the Bread Loaf Barn had been renovated. Additional classrooms were built downstairs, and a large open dormitory for men was provided upstairs. Dean Harry Owen assigned all the men students on scholarships to the Barn dormitory. But even before classes began on July 1, it was obvious that the open dormitory was far too noisy and public for studying and sleeping. I spoke with Harry Owen, and he arranged for me and another student, Richard Ellmann, to move to Gilmore Cottage, and we roomed together there for the summer. Dick Ellmann already had his Ph.D. from Yale University and was a published poet, and he had come to Bread Loaf to work with Ted Morrison, hoping to secure a teaching position in the freshman English program at Harvard as the first step in his academic career. In this he succeeded.

One afternoon very late in June I visited Frost at the Homer Noble farm to arrange for an evening of "good talk." Frost had come up to Ripton much later this summer. He looked in excellent physical shape and had obviously recovered from the emotional shock of his son's death. His farm appeared more flourishing than ever before, with the addition of a horse and a cow and the loud cackling of several hundred chickens. I returned that evening at sunset, and we went up to the cabin. I remarked that since this was my third summer on the Mountain I was fast becoming an "old timer" at Bread Loaf. Frost laughed and responded that he had been coming to Bread Loaf for twenty years and the native Vermonters still regarded him as "summer people." He was accepted at Bread Loaf because the faculty and students were themselves summer people, and besides they all shared the common bond of literature. Frost praised the many good literary and academic traditions blended together among the faculty and students at Bread Loaf. It was good that the Bread Loaf School ran for only six weeks. He wondered whether its virtues would be sustained beyond that length of time. It was that very rare thing—a Brook Farm that worked, without the drudgery and tyranny of a commune. In contrast to the School, the Writers' Conference was more a "Panti-socratic society" rooted in writing, rather than in academics and philosophy. Two weeks was the right length for the Conference.

I remarked that I hoped to have the best of both worlds that summer, since I had signed up for Ted Morrison's "Seminar in Writing," George F. Thomas's "The Platonic Tradition in English Literature," and a course taught jointly by John Crowe Ransom and Theodore Meyer Greene, "The Critical and Philosophical Approaches to Literature." Frost said he hoped I would keep to a poetic approach to poetry and never forget that poetry is a literary art and not a means to advance philosophy or anything else. The themes or content of poetry were often philosophical, but poetry did not consist in *what* was said but *how* it was said. In his myths Plato used the techniques of poetry to illuminate his ideas, but he was too committed to abstract reason, to the world as understood by reason, to be anything but a philosopher. Yet at times, as a mythmaker, Plato was also a poet, and he understood the power of poetry so well that he feared for philosophy, feared that poetry would displace it in the world. Since Plato's whole object was to leap from the physical world to the metaphysical Being of philosophy he was right to use myths, since reason alone was not capable of such a leap.

Frost remarked that we often hear people tell how Plato stands for just one thing, but he stands for many things. Frost told of an encounter he once had about Plato with a college professor friend. The professor insisted that Plato meant only a certain particular thing, and when Frost disagreed, he said: "I know what the trouble is with you. You're a poet, and you know what Plato thought about poets." That was very unfair, Frost remarked, because in reading Plato he was a man before he was a poet. He read Plato as he read anyone else, as himself, not as a member of any one group. Frost insisted that he was himself as a man first, before he was a member of any group, profession, or nation. Plato was most the philosopher in the *Republic,* but he was more poet than philosopher in the *Symposium,*

Ion, and *Laws.* The professor either didn't know this, or ignored the poet in Plato. Reason was Plato's metaphor, which is why his understanding of Form is so abstract, so far removed from the reality of the senses. I was confident that Frost was not a Platonist, but to confirm my conviction I asked whether he was in any sense a Platonist. Frost replied that he believed in the immanence of the reality of physical presences perceived by the senses more than in a metaphysical transcendence rationally perceived. He had already said this: "Earth's the right place for love:/I don't know where it's likely to go better" (p. 122). As poets we shape the world from our sense of it, what our senses tell us about it. That is our primary reality, the physical, but it does not exclude the metaphysical. Plato made the metaphysical primary, which is why he was more philosopher than poet. Our earth-anchored Platonists are Utopians; they want their heaven on earth. Frost concluded his remarks on Plato by repeating that Plato was many things, that it was hard to get away from Plato, try as we might.

Frost said the real value of the courses I was taking would not be in the body of knowledge I learned, but in the skills I acquired, in the ongoing process of self-development. I indicated a book I had brought with me and told him I was still reading Dryden's poetry, as an outgrowth of my course last summer with Reuben Brower. Frost remarked that Dryden and Pope were our best poets since Horace in using irony and allusion as metaphors of language. The iambic pentameter couplet as a verse form was their metaphor of form. It was ideal for reflective poetry or for brief aphorisms. The couplet as metaphor was the closest thing he retained in salvaging parts of a poem that failed. In his reflective poems he allowed himself to revise lines as couplets. If he could steal a good couplet out of a poem he couldn't write, and include it so naturally in a poem that the joint didn't show, he had no qualms about it. But it was a rare occurrence. It had happened in "Birches," but he wasn't even sure now in which lines.

Frost asked me what of Dryden I had been reading. I had just finished "Religio Laici" and the first part of "The Hind and the Panther." I remarked that they were nonlyrical in tone, rhetorical reflective poems, strong in stating philosophical and religious themes. In each poem I had noted a passage that reminded me of Frost's theme in "The Death of the Hired Man," on the conflict-between the claims of justice and mercy, as made by Warren and Mary regarding Silas, their hired man.

Frost responded that "the justice-mercy dilemma" had concerned him for a long time, and he was curious about Dryden's views. I had already marked the two passages, and read first the lines from "The Hind and the Panther," in which Dryden described the two unique qualities God compounded into human nature at the time of man's creation, divine qualities which distinguished man from all other animals:

> But when arrived at last to human race,
> The Godhead took a deep consid'ring space;
> And, to distinguish man from all the rest,
> Unlock'd the sacred treasures of his breast;
> And mercy mix'd with reason did impart,
> One to his head, the other to his heart:
> Reason to rule, but mercy to forgive:
> The first is law, the last prerogative.
>
> (Part 1, 11. 255-62)

While I was hunting for the passage from "Religio Laici" I observed Frost slowly nodding his head in approval of what I had just read.

He noted that Dryden set "reason" rather than "justice" against mercy, and that he left unanswered the crucial question of which of the two should prevail. He said the passage was not as biased in favor of mercy as was Portia's speech in *The Merchant of Venice.* I remarked that I thought Dryden answered the question in one sense in this passage in "Religio Laici":

> But if there be a pow'r too just and strong
> To wink at crimes,, and bear unpunish'd wrong;
> Look humbly upward, see his will disclose
> The forfeit first, and then the fine impose:
> A mulct thy poverty could never pay
> Had not eternal wisdom found the way
> And with celestial wealth supplied the store:
> His justice makes the fine, his mercy quits the score.
>
> (11. 99-106)

I shall never forget the sudden startled expression which leaped to Frost's face, and the manner of his response to this passage. He sat bolt upright in his Morris chair and almost shouted: "That's it!" Dryden has reconciled the Old and the New Testament." It answers why men need to look up to God as the final power and arbiter, whose will and wisdom reconciled justice and mercy in judging men. Frost asked to see the two passages and I gave him the book. After he had read them over slowly he noted that in "The Hind and the Panther" Dryden had remained neutral while he mixed "reason" and "mercy" in man, but in "Religio Laici" he had God's will and mercy triumphant over His justice. I asked Frost what that signified. He replied cryptically that it put Dryden closer to St. Augustine than to St. Thomas Aquinas.

Frost argued that there is a natural conflict built into the moral universe between justice and mercy. We see it clearly in how men respond to even the most serious violations of the criminal law. Those who favor capital punishment for murder believe more in justice than in mercy; those who oppose capital punishment believe more in mercy than in justice. Frost remarked that in our age there is danger of destroying justice between men in the name of mercy for all men. This applies to more than the criminal code. In economics mercy is often made to triumph for the poor in the name of distributive justice, which is really injustice to the rich. The redistribution of wealth is becoming more and more the main function of the state. We have "an unholy alliance" between "New Testament Christian sapheads," who take the Sermon on the Mount as having cancelled out the Law of Moses in some of its prohibitions, and sentimental humanitarians, who believe that all the evil in the world is caused by a bad arrangement of social machinery. These religious and secular groups combine to make mercy prevail over justice. Frost said that as the idea applies to God rather than man, they have Milton on their side. In *Paradise Lost* Milton wrote of God: "But mercy first and last shall brightest shine" (Book III, 1. 134). Frost said, "Please note, *first and last.*"

Frost remarked that he was talking recently to a Unitarian minister, who said his congregation could be divided into two groups— "theists and humanitarians." Frost said that what the minister really meant, though he couldn't bring himself to say it, was "theists and atheists." The first group is in a direct line of descent from Emerson and Channing, idealistic transcendentalists, believers in an "Over-soul," etc. The second group is really secular, recognizes no revelation beyond science and human reason, no Godhead, and believes in the "brotherhood of man." They are "realists rather than idealists," not because they will realize what they want, nor because matter is more real than spirit, but because what they are working with and working for seems tangibly real to their senses. Frost remarked that the "theists" among the Unitarians are really Universalists. They start with God and believe that God is too good to damn any man and that therefore all men will be saved. Salvation is universal. The "humanitarian" Unitarians start with man and believe that men are too good to be damned by any God, if He exists. So they also end up believing in universal salvation, but in a secular rather than a religious sense. I asked Frost what he believed about all this theology. He refused to commit himself to anything. Finally, in a very wary manner, he depersonalized my question and said that none of us deserves salvation, but all men hope to have it. I could see that the subject of salvation was one which agitated Frost's heart, and he was unwilling to put a public label on his private convictions concerning it.

I expressed great wonder how Unitarianism, which preached universal salvation for man, could have derived from Calvinism, which preached "universal depravity" and damnation for all mankind except God's "elect," who were His chosen few. Frost gave the opinion that somewhere between the time of Calvin and that of Emerson the Calvinist doctrine of grace must have been turned inside out, so that either God's "elect" came to include more and more of mankind, or "universal depravity" came to be more and more restricted until even the worst villains and unbelievers were not included.

After a long pause, in which Frost allowed his opinion to register in my mind, he got onto an old familiar subject—Puritanism. Frost expressed his belief that Milton's *Comus* was the greatest Puritan poem ever written. I said that I would have voted for Spenser's *The Faerie Queene.* Frost said there was too much sensuality in Spenser. I perceived that after two years there were still some differences between us regarding Puritanism. According to Frost Milton's greatness as a man and a poet rested on his faith in himself and in his moral courage. His best poems are his shorter, earlier ones, and *Samson Agonistes,* but in *Paradise Lost* Milton proved his courage to the world. Wasn't it a thing to marvel at, Frost remarked, that the two greatest epics in our literature were composed by poets who were blind. What incredible feats of courage Homer and Milton performed. Frost's voice became filled with pathos as he said: "Isn't it a sad world when courage is the supreme virtue in man?" I objected that for a poet talent must be supreme, because without talent all the determination in the world would not get him anywhere. Frost conceded that talent was essential, yet he insisted that the reverse was also true—that talent without courage would not make a poet. Without courage all of our other virtues, including our literary talents, become merely theoretical. Writing a poem is primarily an act of self-faith and courage. And failure in writing is largely the result of a lack of faith and courage. No real agnostic could ever write a true poem, said Frost. Writing the first line of a poem involves a commitment by the poet, and every line thereafter is an act of disciplined will, of courage and faith that he can run the whole course to the finish line and believe the poem into existence. When young writers quit, it is most often a failure of nerve, not of talent.

Frost extended his argument on courage beyond literature to the whole of life. Men should be firm and courageous in their commitments in everything—in love and marriage, in religion, art, politics, and loyalty to their country and their friends. Agnosticism paralyzes the will and makes men cowards. Better a convinced theist or atheist than an agnostic. I remarked that John Henry Newman compared being an agnostic to standing on one leg forever. Frost responded that that was what our political agnostics, the liberals, often did. They couldn't make up their minds and therefore were weak and indecisive as leaders. It was no excuse to say that we didn't know enough yet to take a firm position. It isn't a question of knowing, but of believing and acting. Even the best informed men act from insufficient knowledge; often we can believe our knowledge into existence sufficiently well to take action. Agnosticism is a miserable kind of neutrality about the most crucial questions of life and death.

Our talkathon lasted well beyond midnight, when Frost took his lantern and guided me down his dirt road to the highway. Although we talked about literature, and Frost had occasion further to expound his favorite themes about voice tones in poetry, it appeared to me that since two summers ago a new dimension of moral philosophy and religion had been added to his literary and political interest. This impression was confirmed during the course of the summer of 1941.

II

The Bread Loaf School was opened by Stephen A. Freeman, Acting President of Middlebury College while President Moody was in

Washington, D.C., as an adviser to the government. The war in Europe was already reaching the Mountain. Two days after classes began, on July 3, Frost gave his annual poetry reading to the 231 students and faculty. Dean Harry Owen introduced him.

Frost read several of the public's favorites among his poems, and made brief comments on several poems. After reading "The Bear" he remarked that we haven't gone much beyond Plato and Aristotle in our thinking in the liberal arts. "Fire and Ice" elicited a reflection that there was "more passion than petrifaction now in the world." "The Demiurge's Laugh" he described as his "first poem on science." He read "The Generations of Men," and said that although pride in ancestry was a fine thing, the old New England Yankee stock sometimes made too much of the Pilgrims. Recent emigrants to America were also pilgrims in their way. Frost told a story of a Polish boy in a small New England town who outstripped everyone in school. He did so well that the old Yankee families were put out by his superiority. They invented a story that the boy must be illegitimate, that he had a Yankee father. They couldn't accept the idea that the son of Polish emigrants could have more ability than the children of old Yankee families.

The dramatic highlight of Frost's poetry reading followed after he read "Not All There":

> I turned to speak to God
> About the world's despair;
> But to make bad matters worse
> I found God wasn't there.
>
> God turned to speak to me
> (Don't anybody laugh);
> God found I wasn't there—
> At least not over half.

Frost addressed his Bread Loaf audience directly and asked whether anyone knew how God got His name. After a long pause the poet said that in the beginning He didn't have a name, and He felt keenly that something was lacking, especially after He had decided to create Earth and man. In creating the earth He took a giant cauldron and built a fire under it. Then He mixed in all the ingredients which were to comprise the earth. And a steam rose from the cauldron, so that

He couldn't quite see what He was doing. But He kept on dumping in more ingredients and stirring the cauldron, and more steam rose from it. At last He became curious to see what kind of mixture He had concocted. As the steam cleared off, He looked over the edge of the cauldron into the bubbling mess and gasped, "God!" And that's how He came to be called "God."

The reaction to Frost's anecdote was decidedly mixed. Those who sensed that he was being puckishly whimsical, and treating God in a spirit of play, laughed with good nature. Malicious free thinkers, who thought Frost was denigrating God, laughed in derision. Pious, humorless, religious souls, who felt Frost was being sacrilegious, stirred uneasily in their seats but did not laugh. Frost sensed that his whimsical anecdote had missed fire among many of his listeners. He shifted gears and suddenly became quite serious.

By definition, if not by name, said Frost, God is that by which we explain all things. We can't explain God, because He is a mystery, but we explain things through God. We believe in God as theists; or we stand forever wondering about Him as agnostics; or disbelieve in Him as atheists. Belief, or faith, is the whole basis of knowledge and understanding of God. And men's belief has important practical consequences in their lives. The reason so many people fear death is that they don't understand what God is. God is the One; not any one, but "the ever-ready One." Everything begins and meets in "the ever-ready One." Most people don't think seriously about death until they find themselves in a hospital, or in an old folk's home weaving baskets. Frost concluded his remarks by saying that every time he passed a hospital he sensed the smell of death, and his mind wandered up and down the corridors.

After Frost's poetry reading many students went to the Barn and debated his remarks about God and death until well past midnight. I found myself in the small minority who understood Frost as a theist whose faith in God allowed room for a comic treatment of the deity.

III

On the following Sunday afternoon, July 6, the Methodist church in Ripton celebrated its sesquicentennial, and as Bread Loafers were invited I attended. The featured speakers were Bill Meacham, a graduate of Middlebury who had spent many summers in Ripton; Robert

Noble, a native of Ripton; and Robert Frost. The poet's grandson, Prescott Frost, around seventeen years old, was in the audience. He had an uncanny physical resemblance to his grandfather. I saw him again at several Friday night square dances in Ripton during July, and each time he made me think that Frost as a teenager must have looked like him.

Frost spoke briefly on how the Hebrew Old Testament provided the basis for the Christian New Testament. His theme was that Christ had fulfilled the Decalogue which Moses had delivered to the Jewish people, providing a new spirit for the letter of the moral law in the Sermon on the Mount. He noted that when Moses came down from the mountain to deliver the Ten Commandments to God's chosen people, even before he could give them the stone tablets he found them violating the first and most important law by worshipping and dancing around the golden calf they had made. In his anger Moses threw down the tablets, and they were broken. This symbolized that the moral laws are always being broken. To this day, he noted, over the entrance of synagogues the Ten Commandments are chiseled in stone, with a crack running across the tablets. The greatest troubles suffered by Jews and Christians occur when they are false to their covenants and reject the revelations of their religion.

Frost's words were well-received by his Ripton audience. His undoubted orthodoxy in religion was clearly evident on this occasion, in contrast to his ambiguous raillery about God three days earlier.

IV

On two other occasions during July I visited Frost at his cabin with student friends; once with Laura Woodard, a student from Vanderbilt University studying at Bread Loaf; and once with George Sullivan, Charley Cotter, and Howard Friedman, friends from Middlebury College. The first talk remained on the social level and produced no serious talk on politics, literature, education, science, or religion—the subjects that really interested Frost. Although the second talk got into some significant matters concerning Emerson, it was dissipated by having too many focal points among Frost's listeners. I concluded after that evening that in the future I would come alone.

Frost expressed his conviction that Emerson was a fine poet and prophet, but not a great philosopher, particularly if we include as poetry some passages of his prose. Indeed, Emerson was really not a philosopher. He was an intuitionalist and a leaper, not a plodding logician. It would be hard to reduce his themes and arguments about things metaphysical to any systematic or coherent form. There are large gaps in his theories and considerable confusion. This didn't bother Emerson much. That was his happy fault. Emerson was a great phrasemaker and symbolist, because he saw the whole of nature; and the facts and particular objects of nature were to him symbols in God's divine plan of the universe. As a poet Emerson fused form and soul in metaphor. At times he was a bit oracular, a priest-poet. There are many good ideas and insights in Emerson's essays, particularly in *Representative Men,* but he is essentially a poet.

Someone asked whether Frost thought Emerson was as good a poet as Emily Dickinson. Frost said both are excellent poets; both are concise and aphoristic, and have a profound sense of form. Dickinson was our best woman poet by far, probably the best ever in Western civilization—better than Sappho, Elizabeth Barrett Browning, or even Christina Rossetti. But, said Frost, toward the end of her life Emily Dickinson was "quite mad." Her garden and home became her universe, and she turned inward more and more. With Emerson it was the other way around. He turned outward from himself and tried to thrust his mind to reach the farthest points of the universe. He knew that all rays return upon themselves and end in the human mind. The more powerful the mind, the more it could penetrate into matter and space. Emerson's expansiveness is concentrated; by contrast, Whitman's is diffused.

Someone else asked what was weakest about Emerson as a philosopher. Frost replied that Emerson's moral theory was monistic. Evil was the absence of good, not a reality in itself. Emerson explained evil by explaining it away. He was too optimistic by far about human nature. He had imbibed the theory of progress in history. Emerson saw only "the good of evil born, but not the evil born of good." Frost asked where in Emerson we could find "the good of evil born," and luckily I identified it as from "Uriel." Frost remarked that the angel Uriel was an orthodox rebel who tried to raise conventional morality to a higher level of understanding than the literalness of the later Pharisees, back to the spirit of the prophets. The original Pharisees were not pharisaical.

V

On Friday, July 25, at the request of Harry Owen, Frost came to the campus to speak on teaching reading and writing in high school, to Bread Loaf students who taught high school English. He seemed to take his point of departure from a lecture Louis Untermeyer had given at Bread Loaf on July 14, on "How to Hate Poetry." Frost attacked analytical criticism of poetry and said that such critics are to poetry what the scribes and Pharisees were to Scripture. He objected to reading assignments which treated poetry as anything other than an art form, as an adjunct of science, history, grammar, or argument. He objected to assignments in source studies or "borrowings." A poem should not be judged by where a poet got his ideas or plot. A poet should be judged by his performance, by what he did with what he borrowed. If students are simply exposed to poetry good poems will dawn in their minds like the dawn of a new day. This happens best not by making a paraphrase of a poem, but by applying the central metaphor to a familiar situation in life. By combining books and life in reading assignments teachers can illuminate two kinds of truth for their students: learning something they knew but had forgotten, which is common in experience; and learning something new, which is rare in experience. Both truths are forms of insight rather than of knowledge. Most students know what they have learned in the order in which they learned it. A teacher should show them how much better it is to get at the premises of ideas in their readings. Frost gestured with his index finger to stress his main points. He said several times: "Never forget the fun of play in reading."

Frost turned from teaching reading to teaching writing. He insisted that a teacher should never assign exercises in writing. Let the students be free in spirit to write what they will, immediately, as well as they can. And never mind mechanics and syntax. If students read with care they will pick up correct usage as they go along; and if they don't, it doesn't matter, because they won't be writers anyway. Teachers who insist on preciseness in mechanics and grammar are big in little things and little in the great virtues in writing—initiative, daring, originality. It is ironical that these mere linguists and mechanists parade their authority and assume to themselves the public image of a teacher of English. They are often majestic in their self-importance. But it's a miserly mistake for a teacher to keep the sleeping spirit in a child sleeping too long. The high school English teacher's job is the same as Prince Charming's, to awake the Sleeping Beauty with a kiss. Prince Charming didn't waste time trying to spoon feed the Sleeping Beauty before he awakened her. From the first writing assignment students should be made aware that their own experiences and ideas are the most vital thing that can engage their minds and hearts in what they have to say. It is important that every student is taught to do his very best every time he writes, to extend himself to his utmost limits, to make his words stand forth as deeds. If necessary, do something shocking and dramatic to get this point across to students. Frost told an anecdote—when he taught English at Pinkerton Academy, in Derry, New Hampshire, he held up a set of papers his students had written and asked: "Is there anything here that anyone wants to keep permanently?" No one said yes, so he shouted to the class: "I am not a perfunctory reader of perfunctory writing," and threw the papers in the waste basket. An indefinable murmur passed through the audience as Frost finished his story.

Frost argued that student aspiration counts for far more than teacher inspiration of students. No one can prod someone else into being a writer. If prodding can create writers why don't the teachers prod each other? He challenged his audience: "Have you ever wondered why so few teachers of English can write well?" Teachers and students would do well to prod themselves. Aspiration is really self-belief. A poet believes and wills himself into existence as a poet. He will know he is a poet before anyone else knows it, but modesty forbids him to announce it to the world. He must wait until the world recognizes it and calls him a poet. A young man who has published a poem or two in a school magazine is hardly qualified to be called a poet, any more than a boy who signs up to become a seminarian should be called a priest. For both poetry and the ministry, many are called but few are chosen.

In teaching we get most from a student not by putting the screws on him but by our example, our presence as a teacher, challenging him to his best efforts, like a coach on the athletic field. We should know in teaching not to teach. There has been much recent nonsense that the student, rather than the teacher, should decide what and how learning should take place. That is to deny that experience has any value in life or in wisdom about life. Youth must go to school to their elders.

Frost emphasized that to write is to think, to have original thoughts by putting together impressions, ideas, and sensations that have never before been combined. To think is to create images, make analogies, and perceive metaphors. When a student succeeds in doing these things he knows it immediately; he does not have to wait a week or a month to know that he has said better what he has never before thought or said as well. He knows intuitively when what he has written is good, just as he knows when he falls in love that the object of his love is good. He knows it the way an archer knows when his arrow strikes the bullseye. He may lack taste and judgment, but these will come in time as he grows. And as a member of society he wants and needs the praise and approval of his teachers and friends.

To illustrate the danger of expecting praise too soon from their teachers, Frost told an anecdote about two green-eyed fishermen. The poet said that young would-be writers often came to him and showed him their work and expected him to tell them they were going to be writers. He generally told them the story of the green-eyed fishermen. It goes like this. Two fishermen lived by a lake, and whenever they wanted some fish they would paddle out to the middle of the lake in their small boat, and one fisherman would say to the other: "Are my eyes green?" "No, not yet," the other would say. Then they would paddle around some more and the first one would say, "Are my eyes green now?" The second fisherman would say, "Yes they're green now." And the first one would dive in and catch some fish. Then one day the two fishermen went out in the lake to catch fish and the first one asked: "Are my eyes green?" "No, not yet," the second answered. After they had paddled around a little more the first one said, "Are my eyes green now?" The other answered, "No, not yet." Then the first one said, "Oh, come on now! Say that my eyes are green." Then the second one said, "All right, then, your eyes are green." Whereupon the first fisherman dove into the lake and was drowned. Frost remarked that that is the way it is with so many young would-be writers: they all want to be told that their eyes are green.

Frost mused that often young would-be poets read a poem to him and that if he didn't say anything about it they thought he didn't like it and felt they must say something in the poem's defense. Often in explaining the poem they said things that were better than the poem itself. The poet said he often discovered at this point that the poem was assigned by a teacher, while the remarks about the poem were "self-assigned," and came from the student. According to Frost, writing a poem should be self-assigned, so that the poem unfolds itself as naturally as the opening lines of Keats's *Hyperion*. But before a young writer can write well with ease he must discipline himself by learning to use his tools. Before a young writer can experience anything like the intuition in Keats's "wild surmise" he must have a keen sense of the range of meanings possible in the sounds and rhythms of the English language, and he must know by immediate sense recognition the chief verse forms.

Frost spoke at length of meter, rhythm, and the sound of meaning in poetry. He asserted that "there is only one meter in English poetry, the iambic, more or less loose or strict." A line of English verse is seldom more than five feet, as it often is in Latin poetry. We can't be too precise or scientific about meter and rhythm. Robert Bridges had a theory about meter in English poetry which would have made it as dead to us as Latin is a dead language to most English-speaking people. Bridges's friend Gerard Manley Hopkins tried to do the same thing with rhythm—what he called "sprung rhythm"— that Bridges did with meter. Hopkins's loose rhythm is too contrived, whether viewed as theory or in his own practice as a poet.

In reading a line or passage of poetry out loud, Frost remarked, there should be no need or reason to consciously stress one word or phrase more than another, in order to make a point. The stresses should come naturally, from within the word itself, as it were, as if one were speaking common idiomatic English. To illustrate his point Frost quoted a line from "Birches," "It's when I'm weary of considerations," and asked: "Which word is naturally stressed in that line?" If the dramatic effect is to emerge out of the situation of the speaker in the monologue, rather than being put on it from without by the reader, the word "weary" must receive heavy stress. Frost dragged out the middle vowel sounds until they approached being two syllables. By stressing the word "weary" thus, the character speaks in his own true psychological response to his condition. The sound conveys the dramatic meaning, just as in onomatopoeia the sound of a word imitates an action. Frost mentioned *hiss, buzz, whirr* and *whirl, slam, suck,* and *sizzle,* as examples of words in which the meaning is carried in the sound. Meter alone is too limited and monotonous to convey meaning through sounds. To create "the tune of a poem" the variations in rhythm must cut across the relatively fixed meter. Rhythm provides the range of meanings in a poem. Frost's example for this was to imagine two people arguing in a room, whose voices could be heard rising and falling, even though no distinct words could be made out. A listener would get a very good idea of what was meant by each voice in the argument, even without hearing the words, through the pitch and the rhythm. It is a common mistake, said Frost, to think of metaphor as only a figure in a verse or stanza. The common verse forms are themselves metaphoric. A blank verse lays down a direct line of image, thought, or sentiment. The couplet contrasts, compares, or makes parallel figures, ideas, and feelings. The quatrain combines two couplets alternatively. The sonnet gives a little drama in several scenes to a lyric sentiment. All of these verse forms have their possibilities and limitations in providing a poet with his means to strip life to form and fix the flux of life for a moment permanently in language. Poetry is not "an escape" from life, as so many people seem to think, but a "pursuit of life," a deeper probing into it, and into ourselves, than ordinary everyday living provides. Comedy and tragedy provide the spirit and style of how we take ourselves in the verse forms we use. Frost said that if we write with obvious outer seriousness, there should always be a subtle core of inner wit or humor; and if we write with outer humor or wit, the inner core should always have a serious theme. To leave out half of life is to make poetry less real rather than more real than life. Only silly, thoughtless people, literal-minded boobs, believe in the slogan "more truth than poetry." They assume that the common verse forms are artificial, not found in life as lived by mundane people, and therefore poetry can't present what is true and real in life. Some writers think this way too. They think they have to dredge the dregs of human depravity to write about what is "real." Their "realism" is "sewer realism," Frost punned. To prove that their potato is "real" they have to give us a peck of dirt with it; Frost said he was content to offer his potato brushed clean. All this concerns the style of content or meaning in the common verse forms. The best way for students to learn these forms is to read much English and American poetry, until they have assimilated the forms and made them second nature. Then when they write they will not think of it as "creative writing," a bad, much abused phrase, Frost said, but as "natural." There were no questions from his listeners, and thus the session ended.

VI

On Sunday evening, August 10, Robert Frost and Louis Untermeyer came to Bread Loaf to hear a program of songs by the famous singer Harriet Eells, a mezzo-soprano of the American Opera Company, from Cleveland, Ohio. During the early forties Miss Eells spent several weeks each summer on the Mountain, preparing her recitals for the coming year in Europe and America. She was a strong, striking woman, with a clear, pleasing, powerful voice, and she completely dominated her accompanist, the well-known Hungarian pianist, Arpad Sandor. After singing some German lieder and folk songs, Miss Eells concluded her program by singing several poems by Frost which had been set to music—"The Pasture," and "Stopping by Woods on a Snowy Evening." I could see that Frost was clearly displeased by these song versions of his poems. He liked Miss Eells, and considered her a fine singer, but after the program he did not congratulate her or speak to her about his poems. On July 23 Madame Elizabeth Schumann had given a recital of German lieder at Bread Loaf, and John Crowe Ransom had expressed his dislike of her singing as "too Romantic," because she had tried to charm her audience rather than letting her art speak for itself. But Harriet Eells was a classical singer, so I doubted that it was her singing that had displeased Frost.

Summer school was over on my birthday, August 12, and that night I visited Frost in his cabin for the last time that summer. I immediately asked him what he thought of Miss Eells's rendering of his poems as songs. He said that a poem is already a song, and to add music to it is to change it into something different from itself, to translate it. He insisted that genuine poetry cannot be translated. He remarked that the Italian word to translate, *tradurre,* had the same root as their word to betray, *tradire.* Frost coined an epigram: "To be translated is to be betrayed." Even at its best, said Frost, "a translation is a stewed strawberry." He was glad he didn't know the foreign languages into which his poems had been translated, because it saved him the pain of hearing them mutilated. It was flattering to hear that someone had translated one of his poems, but it was aesthetically painful to hear a translation. More specifically, I asked why can't good poetry be translated into a song without its essence being lost? Frost replied that there's always a conflict between the meter and rhythm of a poem and the meter and rhythm of music. The meter of a poem may be fitted to music, but the rhythm cutting across the meter cannot. That is what is lost in setting a poem to music. The tone and idiom of the spoken language are lost, and something operatic replaces them. Music and poetry are separate art forms, and cannot be combined. The opera is a bastard art form, attempting to be both music and drama, and being neither. No one takes seriously the dramatic plot of an opera. To like opera we must treat it as music. Frost admitted to disliking opera.

With a mischievous twinkle in his eyes Frost said the only kind of poetry that could be improved by translation is free verse. Did he mean Whitman? I asked. He was glad to include Whitman, whose "free verse" was almost as "loose and distended" and sprawling over his page "without compression" and form as most contemporary writing of free verse. Frost remarked that he had once read a long passage of Whitman to some students who said they admired his poetry and asked whether they thought that was good poetry. After they said they thought it was, he told them he had read every other line. "Can you imagine doing that with Pope?" he asked. But the writer he had in mind was Carl Sandburg. Once in the early 1920s, when Sandburg had read his poems at the University of Michigan, Frost said he had thought then that Sandburg accompanied himself on his "geetar" to hide the fact that his free verse had no metrical pattern, only a very loose rhythm. The occasional twangs on the strings supplied the missing meter.

Speaking of the University of Michigan reminded me of the talk we had had with Barbara Fleury last summer, and I asked Frost to tell me about his experience at Michigan. He said he had been the first American poet to be appointed "poet-in-residence" at a university; this had occurred in 1921-22 and was repeated the next year. He was pleased that other colleges and universities have since then had poets- and writers-in-residence; it showed that schools recognize the importance of the arts. I asked him what his duties were at Michigan. Unlike earlier at Amherst, he said, where he was really a teacher and not a poet-in-residence, he had no set courses to teach at Michigan. "I was a poetic radiator," Frost said; "I just sat around and radiated poetry." But, ironically, his freedom from fixed academic duties had been largely negated by the heavy demands of his social life. Such friends as President Marion Burton, Dean Joseph Bursley, and Professors Morris Tilley, Louis Strauss, and Roy Cowden in English, and others, had constantly invited him and his wife out to dinner, afternoon teas, lectures, etc., and he was more a social lion than a poet. Also, the students would frequently invite themselves into his home. He enjoyed talking with them, particularly the staff on the *Whimsies,* but the result was that he neglected to write as much poetry as he wished. His danger was the opposite of that of such poets as Browning and Robinson, who late in life wrote much from habit and fell into the danger of writing commonplace poetry. His danger was that he would dry up.

Did he write anything while in Ann Arbor? I asked. When he returned to Michigan a third time after an interval of another year at Amherst, he lived in a house which he called "chicken Classical," because it had a wing on each side and columns in the middle section. Frost said that this house was later bought by Henry Ford and moved to Greenfield Village, where it is part of that "outdoor museum." He wrote two poems while living in that house, "Spring Pools" and "Acquainted with the Night." He got three lines of "Acquainted with the Night" in an intuitive flash one night while walking alone, when he looked up through some mist or fog at the clock high in the tower of the old Washtenaw County Courthouse:

> And further still at an unearthly height
> One luminary clock against the sky
>
> Proclaimed the time was neither wrong nor right.

The whole sonnet had followed from that intuition, just as after he had written "New Hampshire," staying up all night, at dawn the whole of "Stopping by Woods on a Snowy Evening" had come to him in a flash—all except the next to the last line. Later, he had another intuition that all he had to do was repeat the last line to complete the poem. The actual writing of "Stopping by Woods on a Snowy Evening," Frost said, took him only as long as it took to put the words on paper. But in fact he had *lived* the poem for many years before he wrote it. It had simmered quietly for a long time, then suddenly came to a boil.

The University of Michigan had treated him extremely well, Frost remarked. He had nothing but fond memories of it, and among the large universities in the nation he considered it one of the very best. The Hopwood awards in writing were unique, and the writing program made Michigan much less purely academic than most schools. He could have stayed on for the rest of his life, but it would have been his death as a poet. But he finally learned from going to Michigan that his only real permanent home was New England.

From his first year in Ann Arbor Frost recalled one poet in whom I then had a strong interest. He had persuaded the literary students at Michigan to invite a series of poets to the campus, and among them was Amy Lowell. Frost had then known her for over six years, since soon after his return from England early in 1915, when he had visited her in her home in Brookline, Massachusetts, to thank her for having written some favorable criticism about his first two books of poetry. According to Frost, Amy Lowell was "the perpetual show off." She lived in a large sprawling mansion, and when Frost visited her the first time she was talking to some young Spanish poet whom she had befriended. When her servant ushered Frost in, and she became aware that he could see and hear her, she suddenly became very unfriendly to the Spanish poet, and ordered him out. As he was leaving she stuck her fingers up to her nose at him. It was her way of telling Frost that she was the dominant force in any friendship. In private she liked to smoke big black cigars. Whenever she travelled, Frost said, even if it was only for a very short distance, she always took along at least twenty or thirty suitcases. She refused ever to walk any distance and would take a taxi just to cross the street. She liked to boss people around. In Michigan during her lecture, she came out on the stage with a big ball of electric light cord and made Frost and the janitor undo it in front of the audience, while she supervised them and made wisecracks. She put on a vaudeville show whenever she gave a poetry reading.

Despite her liveliness, her outer pleasantness and nastiness, she was a very sick woman during the last years of her life. Frost said Amy Lowell's doctor told him shortly after her death that he had been within quick calling distance of her for a long time, ready to operate on her immediately. About six months before she suddenly died, Frost had invited her to a little party he gave in New York, but she had refused to come. Instead of telling Frost she was too sick to travel, she just said it was too far to go for a party. Frost felt she had snubbed him, so that shortly afterwards when she gave a party to celebrate the publication of her study of Keats and invited Frost, he also refused. Had he known how sick she was, and that illness and not pride or envy had prevented her from attending his party, he would have gone to her celebration. During the last few months of Amy Lowell's life she and Frost were peeved with each other. Frost remarked sadly that he had always been sorry for his part in their alienation.

I asked Frost what he thought of Amy Lowell as an imagist and free verse poet. He remarked that there were two main reasons why many poor poets turned to free verse, apart from its being very easy to write. One group thinks the world picture is too chaotic and dark for any order to be made out of it in the traditional forms of poetry. Therefore, they try to show the world's chaos through free verse. The other group feels that rhymed metrical-cadenced patterns impose too great a burden on them. Arny Lowell belonged to the second group. She was neither a thinker nor a poet, but simply a literary dilettante with a flair for advertising herself.

Frost said he was amused at the inflated literary reputations of some contemporary free verse poets, whose academic admirers praised them by denigrating much better poets who had written in traditional forms. Once during the twenties he was scheduled to give a poetry reading at a socially prestigious Eastern women's college, where he had heard that the professors of English dismissed Longfellow as a sentimental nineteenth-century Eddy Guest. Frost told his audience that before reading from his own poems he would read from the work of a poet he thought they should know. He read several of Longfellow's poems without identifying the author, and each poem was greeted with enthusiasm. When the audience was at a high pitch to know who had written these excellent poems Frost identified him as Longfellow, and a gasp of unbelief went through the coeds. Frost urged the students to read more of Longfellow, and other traditional poets, and to trust their own taste and judgment rather than taking any so-called authority's word about any poet.

There were times during our conversation when I had a unique sense that Robert Frost in the flesh before me, in the flow of his voice, was an imaginary character in a drama of ideas. My role was to ask questions to open the larger drama of life in some future offstage action. I hoped that action would be in my future teaching and writing.

To move to another subject, I quoted Frost's epigram, "Precaution," "I never dared be radical when young / For fear it would make me conservative when old," and asked him whether that wasn't a conservative statement, in that a radical ran to extremes and was without precaution, and a conservative was the opposite? The real extremes, Frost said, would be "revolutionary and reactionary." As abstractions such terms mean little by meaning too much. But most people are a mixture of both—radical in some things and conservative in others. He remarked that he had known religious radicals who were conservatives in education and politics.

Frost then told an amusing anecdote about a group of students at Amherst who thought they were radical, and asked him if he would introduce a speaker of their choice at their next club meeting. Frost agreed to do this. The students had no money so they asked Frost if he knew of any wealthy alumnus who would pay for a speaker. Frost got a local conservative Amherst graduate to provide the money. The students chose Bertrand Russell as the most radical person they could get. Russell had been lecturing at Harvard, advocating free love and mixed dormitories for men and coeds; he was a militant pacifist and very unorthodox in religion. The day that Russell was to give his talk Frost said he received several telephone calls from the students, who feared he would be afraid to introduce such an avowed radical and therefore would leave town. Frost remarked that he introduced Russell by referring ironically to the introduction of his latest book, in which Russell had said that he was publishing it in a hurry before he changed his mind about his theme. Russell was a very gentle-looking English radical, come to shock the moss-backed conservatives of Amherst, who had come to his lecture in trepidation and fear of what he would say. And there, said Frost, in that paneled room of ardent young radical students, waiting eagerly for the bombs to be thrown, Bertrand Russell delivered one of the most timid and conventional speeches he ever heard.

After we had laughed heartily over Frost's story, we drifted into a discussion of the war in Europe. The poet told a story of something he had witnessed last summer at Bread Loaf. Count Carlo Sforza had told Frost and a group at the School of English of an incident that had happened to him before he was driven out of Italy by the Fascists. The Count had been talking politics to a young Italian Fascist, Emilio Martinetti, who had said to him: "The day is past when discussions between nations will settle disputes. The only solution to arguments between countries is the solid blow in the face." To which Count Sforza had replied: "Do you mean like this?" as he suddenly punched Martinetti full force in the face.

Frost said Count Sforza referred to Fascism as "the philosophy of the clenched fist." His point was that civilized nations and individuals talked their way through problems, and did not resort to war. But, said Frost laughing, by literally beating Martinetti to the punch the Count had proved him right. Of course the Count was right initially, because nations should try to settle their differences by peaceful means. Only an idiot nation would go to war for the sake of war. But when serious differences cannot be settled by diplomacy or negotiation, war is the final means of settling conflicts. In war, said Frost, both sides assume that justice is on their side. Each nation assumes it must win to secure justice over its enemy. War, then, is the final proof of a nation's faith in itself and in its courage to meet the conditions of survival and greatness. The pacifists don't understand this or can't accept it. The conditions of life for survival and greatness include strife and war.

Frost said he was glad President Roosevelt was not a pacifist, as Woodrow Wilson was. However much he criticized Roosevelt's "New Deal," he could not fault him about war. Frost expressed concern that if war came to the United States the nation would not be prepared for it, materially and spiritually. "Archie" MacLeish's theme in "The Irresponsibles" showed a turning of the tide against the cynical defeatism following the First World War. If democracy is the best form of government (and it is) then it must find and elevate the best people in order to survive and triumph—the best poets, politicians, generals, leaders, etc. Frost said he was glad Roosevelt had expressed his courage to fight if it became necessary. Despite their terrible losses in prisoners and land, the Russians had stalled the German armies and were beginning to counterattack. This spoke well for them.

Frost then turned his guns on domestic national politics. The great danger in the world at large—the sweep to collectivism—was present in a mild form in the United States. Collectivism, he said, means "all pigging together," which is what Roosevelt's "New Deal" wanted for

Americans. Frost said he didn't believe "truckling to the mob speeds the world's wheels." If Vice President Henry Wallace's slogan was accurate, if this is "the century of the common man," then our individual freedom will be lost. Wallace, like Sandburg, believed in "The People, Yes," but not in "The People, Yes; and the People, No."

Our founding fathers knew better, said Frost. Being more religious they knew that only God had or should have absolute power. Frost expressed great admiration for George Washington because after the American Revolution, when absolute power was offered to him, he refused it in favor of limited power through divided and balanced parliamentary government. Frost said that next to Washington he most admired Madison, for incorporating the division and balance of power principle into the United States Constitution. Frost expressed concern that Franklin D. Roosevelt had destroyed that principle in 1940 in being elected to a third term. He referred to Roosevelt as "a third termite." But he was not happy about Wendell Willkie either, an international pacifist and "one-worlder."

The greatest branch of our government, Frost contended, "was the Supreme Court. He had confidence that it would preserve the American federal-states system long after many other nations disappeared. He didn't always agree with the Supreme Court's decisions, and certainly not with the recent decision upholding the federal statute restricting work for sixteen and eighteen year old youths, and setting hours of labor at a maximum of forty hours per week. He had asked his friend Justice Felix Frankfurter why he had voted to uphold that law. The answer was purely sentimental; it had nothing much to do with law or freedom or labor. Frost said that he asked Frankfurter: "How many hours a week do you work?" Frankfurter had answered: "About seventy or eighty. Oh, but that's different! The poor have nothing else to look forward to." Frost said he had asked Frankfurter how the forty-hours-a-week law would help the ambitious poor who were willing and able to work longer? Wouldn't they just get a second job? Far from helping the self-reliant poor, such a law restricted them from rising from their poverty.

Frost remarked that the state does not create anything: it merely takes through taxes what its citizens create. But then it gives back in a new distribution of wealth. Where before there was only justice or injustice, the state mixes mercy with justice. It can't carry the proportions of mercy and justice too far in favor of mercy without violating the theme of the nursery rhyme about the goose that laid the golden eggs. If it kills the goose, it will not be able to make any more omelets. In our "Robin Hood politics" the state robs the rich to give to the poor. It can't do otherwise, except to leave rich and poor alone. The state can't take from the poor—they have little or nothing to take. It shouldn't give to the rich—they don't need it. The end of every modern government is to create more and more equality of conditions among men. But the great evil is that this is done at the expense of private freedom and justice. The modern socialist state wants a society based on mercy alone. This is impossible. Frost said he favored a society based on justice, but infused with mercy.

I asked Frost why there was always so much corruption in politics. He replied that you don't catch saints going into politics. The saints are contemplatives, not activists. Theirs is the response of character and will to a personal moral dilemma. The best people are morally good without being do-gooders. As Luther said, salvation comes through faith alone. Actions speak softer than prayers to men of faith. Other than saints the best people are good-doers, not do-gooders. That leaves the politicians to do good or do well in society as they see fit. Politics is the seeking out of solutions to social grievances. That involves power and action through statutes and laws. That is why so many lawyers go into politics. In politics, law, power, and money all come together. The premium trait for success is shrewdness, boldness, sociability, prudence, and many lesser virtues that feather off into vices. Manipulating situations leads to swapping favors, patronage, and shyster lawyer tricks: ergo, corruption.

At about two in the morning we took our slow lantern walk down Frost's dirt road to the Bread Loaf highway. It was a particularly pleasant evening. The sky was covered with stars from horizon to horizon, and Frost pointed out and named various constellations. The cool bracing air seemed to put him in an expansive and reflective mood. He expressed his sober confidence that come what may the United States was destined to remain the dominant nation in the world. Our unique constitutional system was still strong, and it would enable us to meet threats from without in war and from within by revolution. Our greatest danger was slow corruption from within through the growth in centralized federal authority. Frost feared the decline of the individual states would also make the American people too reliant on Washington, D.C., with a consequent loss in character and self-reliance. He admired states such as Vermont and New Hampshire, where the old New England Yankee Puritan virtues prevailed. He expected that sooner than we thought—or would wish—the United States would be drawn into the war and that we would prove our mettle as in the past. And, finally, Frost was convinced that American literature would be a match for our power and wealth, as great in the future as in the past. He did not fear for his country.

Frost's words and quiet confidence lifted my spirit. As we shook hands and said good night, I felt closer to him than at any time since we had known each other over the past three summers. As Bread Loafers we had in common our love of poetry. But Frost's love of the United States, his nationalism without jingoism, enlarged and intensified our common identity as Americans. It was more personal than social, like the family feeling that is bred in the bones. Yet Bread Loaf was America at its literary and intellectual best. It was our magic mountain. Its humanized landscape, peopled with the most intelligent, stimulating, and pleasant academicians and professional writers I could wish for, made me aware, that night, through Frost that Bread Loaf was the closest thing to the lost Eden that I would ever know.

VII

The annual gathering of the clan of would-be writers and highland chiefs of the staff at the Writers' Conference of 1941 again found Frost frequently on the Bread Loaf campus. He read his poems, talked to young writers on the West Lawn or in the Barn, played tennis with Kay Morrison, Louis Untermeyer, and Dick Ellmann, autographed books, and regularly took part in the poetry clinics with Untermeyer, who did all the leg work with student manuscripts.

During the School of English session there had been a healthy mixture of academic and literary lectures: Padraic and Mary Colum, Edward Weeks, Louis Untermeyer, professors Irwin Edman (Columbia) and Marjorie Nicholson (Smith), the novelist Julian Green, the poet May Sarton, and the critic Edmund Wilson. Frost had attended only those by his friends. Although he did not attend the special lectures of Elizabeth Drew, a new Bread Loaf faculty member from Cambridge, England, he was well aware through me and several other friends that in her popular course in modern British and American poetry she ranked as the four greatest modern poets Yeats, Eliot, Pound, and Auden, with Frost nowhere in sight. This neat and frail lady with her impeccable clipped English accent was widely accounted one of the leading authorities on modern poetry. She considered "Two Tramps in Mud Time" as Frost's most representative poem. She found it thin and conventional in its fixed stanzas, without anthropological myths, archetypal symbols, or esoteric allusions of the kind found in Yeats, Eliot, and Pound, and without the proletarian social consciousness of Auden. Frost's diction was to her indistinguishable from that of a New England farmer's casual talk. She dismissed Frost as a nineteenth-century relic in the John Greenleaf Whittier tradition of verse. Several years later Miss Drew changed her mind about Frost as a poet, but in 1941 she was the one important anti-Frost dissenter at Bread Loaf.

Apart from Miss Drew, the speakers at the School made easy the transition to the Writers' Conference staff, which included besides Ted Morrison and Frost, such veterans as Walter Pritchard Eaton, John Gassner, John P. Marquand, Fletcher Pratt, and Louis Untermeyer. From the previous summer's staff Edith Mirrielees and Wallace Stegner were absent, but I was delighted to see Barbara Fleury back, and Bernard De Vote also returned after a year away. Frost was very friendly with Marquand and Barbara Fleury, but his relationship with De Voto was clearly cool and strained. Whenever Frost joined a group which included De Voto, his old friend would appear ill at ease and soon would move away by himself. Everyone was aware of their enmity and felt uncomfortable. De Voto stayed at Treman Cottage and spent all his spare time there, rather than around the campus and tennis courts, as in previous years. His closest friend was the petite Fletcher Pratt, wispy in his new beard, about whom there was always a squirrel-like aura. Everyone liked the paradoxical Pratt.

Early in the Conference Frost read his poems in the Little Theatre. He prefaced and interspersed his reading with comments on the war in Europe, and on American politics, very similar to those he had made to me earlier in his cabin. In reading "Mending Wall" he noted that he had gotten the central metaphor of the poem from the idea that human biological life is cellular. The cells of the body constantly break down and are built up again, so that everyone is a wholly new and renewed person every seven years or so. Frost observed ironically that some readers were known to have found political implications in "Mending Wall." He had no objections to that. He noted that good walls are necessary to keep things properly in and properly out. Good walls define good geography, which is necessary for a sound national life. Frost also read "The Bearer of Evil Tidings" and quipped that it contained his version of the Immaculate Conception, oriental style.

But the highlight of Frost's poetry reading was "The Lesson for Today," particularly because the poem was not yet published. It appeared the following year in *A Witness Tree*. After his reading many were convinced that "The Lesson for Today" was an important poem for understanding Frost as a thinker. Like "New Hampshire" it was a reflective poem, in the Horatian tradition, less ironical than "New Hampshire," but more concise and polished in its aphorisms. Frost's contention that it is dangerous to have more knowledge than can be safely assimilated and utilized was well summarized:

> They've tried to grasp with too much social fact
> Too large a situation.

Other outstanding touchstones included some magnificent individual lines:

> The groundwork of all faith is human woe.
> Art and religion love the somber chord.
> Earth's a hard place in which to save the soul....
> We're either nothing or a God's regret.
> One age is like another for the soul.

The final line, "I had a lover's quarrel with the world," was conceded by everyone as a permanent touchstone in the canon of Frost's best lines. Someone prophesied that some day the line would be chiseled in stone on Frost's grave. Indeed, I heard only two listeners voice any dissent about "The Lesson for Today," Cedric Whitman and Theodore Roethke, both Fellows at the Conference, who preferred Frost's lyrics to his philosophical and didactic poems.

After one poetry clinic, a woman who assumed that Frost's poems were autobiographical—not fictional art but personal history—began to discuss one of Frost's lyrics in those terms. He put her in her place with one concise rhetorical question: "When I use the word I in a poem, surely you don't believe I mean ME?"

At the poetry clinics Louis Untermeyer, as usual, could hardly speak a sentence without making a pun. Some of his puns, like his allusion to Shakespeare's "The Merchant of *Venus*," duly elaborated, were quite ribald, like limericks. Frost felt that Untermeyer was rather overdoing his puns and became a bit annoyed with him. To Frost Bread Loaf was neither Bohemian, nor Marxist, nor a place for precious aesthetes, and although he relished good wit and humor as much as anyone, he believed that Untermeyer's clowning sometimes interfered with the serious purpose of the poetry clinics. In light of this fact Frost particularly relished an incident in which I triumphed over Untermeyer. One day while waiting table I was asked to go upstairs with a dinner tray for a sick member of the Conference. As I came back into the dining hall, Louis Untermeyer came past me through the door in company with a lovely Writers' Conferee. He reached into his pocket, pulled out a penny, tossed it nonchalantly on the tray, and said, "Have a tip." When the penny stopped spinning, and I saw the value of the coin, I responded: "Looie, what kind of an animal throws a cent?" Before Untermeyer could come back with a pun or quip, and with the loud laughter of his young partner ringing deliciously in my ears, I slipped past him into the dining hall. Frost remarked on hearing this story that it was good enough to keep "Looie" subdued for a whole morning session.

One of the highlights of the Conference was the guest lecture by William Carlos Williams. His subject was writing poetry "in the American grain," by which he meant to use, or "put over," or "catch," the American vernacular, in the tradition of Whitman. Slang was an excellent source for the diction of poetry, Williams argued. He said that the early Imagistes were really objectivists, content merely to name their subject. But this was not enough for poetry. The present imagists, such as he, aimed to "catch" the idiom of common speech in ways that were diametrically opposed to T. S. Eliot, with his classical allusions. Williams said: "Eliot is a good poet, but he uses the wrong words." Today's imagists don't just *tell* it; they *show* it. A thing that is shown well needs no comment to explain it. Suppose, for example, a cat is lying on a rug and a man comes into the room and deliberately steps on the cat. We don't have to say the man is cruel.

Among his final points Williams said that the sonnet is not a form of poetry, but a word, an obsolete outmoded word. He agreed with what E. E. Cummings was doing with words, splitting them up by syllables, or combining them in new ways, but he favored extending this technique beyond words to include conventional verse forms.

Afterwards I asked Frost what he thought of Williams's argument. Frost replied that some of it was obvious and much of it was dubious. But there was nothing more in the current imagist poetry than there was in their original work back in 1912. Frost was politely unimpressed by Williams.

Wyman Parker, the librarian at Middlebury College, came from Rutherford, New Jersey, Williams's home town, and they had known each other for many years. Parker introduced me to Williams the day after his lecture, and told him I was from Nutley, just across the Passaic River from him. After we had talked about poetry for an hour, Williams invited me to visit him in Rutherford on my trip home after the Writers' Conference, and I accepted. Out of this grew an invitation for Williams to speak at the Middlebury College Literary Club, and a long talk about Ezra Pound, whom Williams knew very well. These were significant epilogues to the Writers' Conference for me and for my third summer at Bread Loaf. But that is another story, just as my five later summers at Bread Loaf, in 1942-44, and 1961-62, are another story.

Since Frost visited Bread Loaf frequently over a period of forty-two years, from 1921 through the summer of 1962, and was after 1938 often there from May or June through September, any balanced understanding of his character and temperament must take into account his life at Bread Loaf—the kinds of activities he engaged in, what he said, whom he knew, how he impressed people, what he liked and disliked. These three pre-war summers of our Bread Loaf talks form but a small part of the total record of the man. It may take years to complete the record. Yet even from the existing incomplete evidence, certain tentative conclusions can be made. There is no question that Frost was one of the greatest conversationalists in all English and American literature, comparable to Dr. Samuel Johnson and Coleridge. His intellectual brilliance is beyond dispute. I learned more from Frost about the nature and function of poetry in my Bread Loaf talks with him than I did from all the professors I ever had, from the B.A. through the Ph.D. What I learned was of immense practical value to me, both as a student and subsequently over decades as a college and university teacher of literature. From Frost's talk I received a conception of poetry and the power of words from which I never recovered. Undoubtedly, Frost's philosophical convictions about religion, politics, education, and science are open to dispute, even when they are clearly ascertained. Yet he presented his principles so brilliantly, and with such wisdom, that even where we may differ from him his position commands intellectual respect.

In addition to his intellectual virtues Frost possessed the social virtues to a very high degree. As a raconteur he had few equals, and his stories almost always carried an important theme. They were generally comic, humorous or satirical, and his spirit of fun and play in telling a good story was often joyous and full of infectious laughter. To hear Frost tell a story was a shared aesthetic experience, and his listeners often ended up laughing as hard as Frost at his punch line; it was never a didactic lesson inflicted by a superior creature on dullards. At such times no one could ask for a more companionable and likeable man than Frost. His skill in putting a visitor at ease included not merely a deep sense of prudence and social tact, but a warm and empathetic feeling toward another person's interests and concerns. It is doubtful that when Frost was candid or caustic in his negative criticism of ideas, events, institutions, or persons, insecurity, envy, or hatred, as has been often asserted without proof, but a philosophical difference between himself and the ideas, institutions, or persons he criticized. For example, throughout his life Frost was thoroughly consistent in his theory of poetry, and this included what he favored and opposed, so that his harsh criticism of the theory and practice of free verse had nothing personal in it, but was directed against free verse regardless of who defended or practiced it. The same may be said regarding his philosophical positions in religion, politics, and education. Behind all of his negative criticism was a positive set of principles he wished to defend. It is no more valid to condemn Frost *as a man* because of his strong criticism of ideas and people he opposed than it would be to castigate Jonathan Swift *as a person* because in his satires he bullwhipped the pride, vices, follies, errors, and bad taste of mankind.

It is a very grave and crude error to separate Frost's or any man's moral nature and psychological or emotional temperament from his intellectual and social virtues. Every Middlebury and Bread Loaf friend of Frost I knew—Vernon Harrington, President Moody, Deans Harry Owen and "Doc" Cook—men who altogether knew him over a period of forty-two years, thought Frost was not only a brilliant man and talented poet but also that he was socially attractive, morally sound, and healthy in his overall harmonious whole. All of these men also agreed that Frost was an extremely intense and emotional man, that his psyche was most complex. Yet this did not prevent them from getting along wonderfully well with Frost. Their relationship with him was not merely professional but personal; there was mutual affection between them. My eight years on the Mountain confirmed to the hilt their view of Frost.

It should be clear that almost everything in my experience of Frost at Bread Loaf contradicts the view of his psychological nature and emotional temperament presented in Lawrance Thompson's three-volume biography. This is neither the time nor the place to examine in any systematic way the portrait of Frost as a man in Thompson's work. But a few basic facts may be noted. Thompson's biography barely mentions Frost at Bread Loaf. A summary sketch of Frost's visits between 1921-36 appears in volume two. In the third volume there is only a brief reference to Frost at the Writers' Conference in 1937; the account of Frost's bad behavior at the Conference in 1938; and a few sentences on a momentary encounter with Bernard De Voto in 1947. And that is all. Twenty-three summers of Frost's life at Bread Loaf are totally omitted by Thompson. Never once does he even mention—much less describe or discuss—Frost's important and intimate relations with the Bread Loaf School between 1938 and 1962, while far less important periods or events receive extensive treatment. At the very least these vital omissions make Thompson's biography terribly lopsided and out of focus.

Much ado is made by Thompson and others of the crisis summer of 1938 in Frost's life, after his wife died, when the poet's so-called "demon" broke loose, when he called himself "a bad man," and was called that by De Voto. The lack of balance and proportion in making this period the basis for understanding Frost as a man is evident in the enormous stress laid on Frost's behavior during this time. Thompson and those who accept him at face value present Frost as a pathologically warped and disturbed man, insecure, childish, petulent, gloomy, filled with despair and nasty guilt feelings of remorse about his family, at times morose and suicidal, and always filled with malicious envy and hatred of contemporary rival poets; in short, a thoroughly disagreeable man, hounded and consumed by his raging "demon." It is significant that in Thompson's index under "Robert Frost," the subject headings are heavily weighted with negative emotional and psychological terms, such as "Badness," "Confusion," "Cowardice," "Death," "Enemies," "Fears," "Hate," "Insanity," "Jealousy," "Sadness," "Self-centeredness," "Suicide," and "Wildness." All of these subjects are in themselves legitimate inquiries in a biography, but very rarely does Thompson provide any opposed or different but positive headings. There is nothing on Frost's "Goodness," "Charity," "Bravery," "Love of Life," "Friends," "Hopes," "Loves," "Sanity," "Benevolence," "Gladness," or "Sociability." Thompson's Freudianism carefully filtered out these traits in Frost as illusory disguises, attempts to conceal the reality of Frost's negative emotions. As a result, the real imbalance in Thompson's biography, stemming from his own Freudian theories, is in his interpretation of the inner nature of Frost, especially his emotional nature. It is ironical that Thompson, who thought of himself as an objective, scientifically rational man and scholar, above the common superstitions of religion, should have created a demonology about Frost.

There is no doubt that Frost had a great ego and much literary vanity, and that the negative emotional traits found in all men, so emphasized by Thompson, existed in Frost in an intense form, larger than ordinary life. But these traits are no more nor any less "real" than their positive opposites, which also existed larger than life in Frost. The specific origins of fears, hatreds, jealousy, etc., are not easily uncovered by the speculative probings of amateur psychoanalysis, which has often been known to attribute to a single simple cause emotional problems which are complex and many-faceted. Undoubtedly, Frost's incredibly difficult personal emotional dilemma derived in general from his early and total commitment to his life of poetry, with all that it entailed in economic sacrifice and emotional suffering in failing to meet his necessary responsibilities to his family. Frost could have avoided this dilemma by never marrying. But he believed in and loved family life as much as poetry, and he paid the terrible price of trying to have both. The personal tragedies which afflicted his family, which had nothing to do with his commitment to poetry, intensified his emotional problems.

My experience of Frost at Bread Loaf, in these three pre-war years, and later, provides some of the positive elements missing from Thompson's biography. Frost's dictum that only those who approached poetry in the true spirit of poetry, and accepted it on its own terms, can understand it and be saved by it, applies as well to individual human beings, and to Frost himself. Thompson approached Frost too much through Sigmund Freud (whom Frost once dubbed "Sigmund Fraud"). I have presented Frost descriptively as a conversationalist, and in the main have allowed him to speak for himself, on his own terms.